# Free to Do Right

## David Field

InterVarsity Press
Downers Grove
Illinois 60515

Second printing
December 1973

© 1973 by
Inter-Varsity Press, London.
First American printing,
June 1973,
by InterVarsity Press,
Downers Grove, Illinois,
with permission from
Inter-Varsity Fellowship,
England. All rights reserved.
No part of this book may
be reproduced in any form
without permission from
InterVarsity Press.

InterVarsity Press is the
book publishing division of
Inter-Varsity Christian
Fellowship.

ISBN 0-87784-549-2
Library of Congress Catalog
Card Number: 73-81577

Quotations from the Bible are
from the Revised Standard
Version (copyrighted 1946 and
1952, Second Edition 1971,
by the Division of Christian
Education, National Council of
the Churches of Christ in the
United States of America), unless
otherwise stated.

Printed in the United States
of America

# Contents

# PREFACE

'Then quite suddenly, just like us,
One got better and the other got wus.' (A. A. Milne)

Doing the right thing is not easy. Even finding out what it is can sometimes be difficult, in spite of the many voices that try to advise us. And there is no shortage of those. 'Make love your aim', says one, 'and don't be hidebound by any set of moral rules and regulations.' 'Obey the Ten Commandments', counsels another, 'and all your problems will be solved.' 'It's good intentions that really count', a third chimes in. Many voices, and all speaking at once.

We live in an exciting world of bewildering complexity and exploding moral values. Old standards are either brushed aside with a smile (along with grandfather's patent remedy for gout), or defended to the last ditch by small anti-permissive organizations. Seldom before has the individual been given so much liberty to make his own moral choices. Toleration covers practically everything, and amid all the hubbub of counter-protests and demands for yet more freedom, the Christian tries to find his way to right moral decisions in the frequently very complicated situations that confront him.

This book is about making moral decisions, and it is intended mainly for Christians, though I hope that those who as yet have no religious faith will find its contents of interest to them too. The main theme is a simple one. If we want to know what 'good' and 'right' are all about, then we must look to God. It is *His* character which expresses true goodness, and *His* will that determines what is right; and neither becomes irrelevant with the passing of time. More-over, it is God who provides men with the moral dynamic they need if they are to achieve the high standards they know they should. In other words, He makes us free to do right.

My chief aim has been to draw out the main guide-lines the Bible provides for those seeking their moral bearings, but at every stage I have tried to 'earth' the argument by direct reference to the moral issues in today's headlines. Inevitably, some of the topics I have included deserve much fuller treatment than I have been able to give them in these few pages, but I hope there is enough here to stimulate discussion and point the way to more detailed study.

I shall always be glad to answer queries readers may have about anything I have written in this book.

*Oak Hill College,*
*Southgate, London N.14.*                    DAVID FIELD

# BEGINNING WITH GOD

Everyone has some moral standard. The terrorist who plants a bomb in the supermarket is doing the right thing according to his scale of values. The relatives of the shoppers who die may disagree with his judgment, but they are entitled to their opinions about morality too. The pleasure-seeker who lounges through life has his own private rules for behaviour, no less than the self-denying community service volunteer who digs wells for villagers in India. Even the man who boasts that he lives without any moral rules and regulations at all, turns out to have his personal rules-of-thumb when it comes to choosing between alternative courses of action in a given situation. And who is to say that his approach to the moral crises of life is better or worse than anybody else's? When we say 'The trouble with life today is that moral standards are *disappearing*', we often really mean 'Life today gets so complicated because moral standards are *multiplying* so fast'.

## Modern moral attitudes

This is not to pretend that twentieth-century conditions have in some way widened the areas of choice. Today, as always, there are three main approaches to moral decision-making.

The first is by observing *rules*. This is the way of maximum security. Rather than make difficult decisions for ourselves, most of us (if we are honest) would prefer to be told in clear-cut terms what is right and what is wrong. It is so much less bewildering to be assured, for example, that telling lies is always bad, than to have to distinguish between black ones and white ones according to the circumstances. The 'rules-only' approach concentrates on the words actually said and the actions actually done. There are no overriding considerations to sway our judgment. We simply classify the incident accurately, and read off the answer in the moral rule-book. It is as simple and straightforward as that. All we need is a source of moral authority that is beyond criticism to write the rules for us in the first place.

The second line of approach focuses on *motives*. To the sensitive decision-maker, the rule-book is an inadequate, blunt instrument for making moral judgments. Most people, for instance, would agree that there is an important distinction to draw between a man who tells an untruth to save his wife's life, and another who falsifies his income tax returns out of selfishness or greed. Or should we attach equal blame to both, because telling lies is always wrong? Clearly it is vital to probe behind words and actions to the motives which inspire them. The key question to ask is not '*What* did X do?', but '*Why* did he do it?'.

The third approach turns our attention to *results*. Rules are useful, the argument goes, but as guide-lines only. Normally getting divorced is a bad thing to do because it destroys a relationship and may jeopardize the security of children. But if circumstances are such that the children's well-being is assured and a happy re-marriage is in the offing, then it is said the general rule may safely be set aside in favour of the likely consequences. So when faced by a moral poser, man's correct reaction is not to run to the rule-book for a set solution, but to weigh up the probable results.

These three approaches are not, of course, mutually exclusive alternatives. Very often motives, results and rules converge to give us unanimous decisions. (I may tell the truth from a good motive, for example, *and* in the belief that honesty pays, *and* because the Ten Commandments tell me not to bear false witness against my neighbour.) Nor does any one of them, by itself, provide a distinctively Christian route to moral truth. John 3: 16 is just one well-known New Testament verse which illustrates the interplay we find in the Bible between all three. God's action in giving His only Son (sacrificial giving is good according to the rule-book) is sandwiched in this verse between a record of His motive (He 'so loved the world') and the good consequences He had in view ('that whoever believes in him should not perish but have eternal life').

The most distinctive feature about modern moral attitudes, however, is their preoccupation with *results* (and, to a lesser extent, with *motives*), to the virtual exclusion of *rules*. As a result, the moral rule-book has become something of a museum-piece. This is no doubt partly a reaction against rigid, legalistic attitudes in the past, and partly a reflection of growing distrust with rule-making authority in the present. If men are cynical about their politicians and agnostic about the existence of a deity, they will inevitably seek a surer foundation for their moral judgments than the laws of a government or the rules of God.

We can see the evidence of this all around us. It is little use, for example, appealing to chapter and verse in any moral code today to combat promiscuity. The only acceptable argument is one which draws attention to the harmful *results* of promiscuous living (and what will we do when VD is no longer a menace?). In a similar way, everyone agrees that the man who gambles away his week's wages on a Friday night is doing a bad thing, but it is not at all so clear that charitable support for the Spastics' football pool comes in the same category. Many would argue that the 'good cause' justifies the gambling. When the rector of a well-known church in Birmingham found that money from the collection-box was being pilfered, the notice he put up did not read 'Thou shalt not steal', but 'As this box is emptied regularly, there is no point in trying to steal from it'. That was a notice full of sound common-sense, but a complete sell-out to the moral spirit of the age.

Some predict that a 'Victorian backlash' in favour of a stricter rule-morality is on the way, but if and when it does arrive the Christian has no automatic reason to rejoice. To him, motives and consequences matter as well as rules. The problem which faces a disciple of Christ today is not how to choose between them, but how to arrive at a correct 'mix' of all three. He needs a moral regulator. Where is he to look?

## The source of goodness

The Bible's answer is crystal-clear. The Christian must look to God. *God* is the source of all goodness. The right action in any situation is the one which conforms to *God's* will. Correct behaviour is *God*-centred behaviour.

Bringing God right into the centre of moral decision-making is such a vitally distinctive mark of Christian ethics that it is worth painting the contrasts in some detail. 'The humanists', declared Anson Mount, religious editor of *Playboy* magazine, 'believe in human welfare and happiness as an end in itself. Christians believe that because we love God, we must love our fellow man. And because we love our fellow man, we must seek his welfare and happiness. It's all the same thing.'

In fact, of course, it is not the same thing at all. The humanist starts with man, while the Christian begins with God. The Bible's moral demands assume that those to whom they are directed are bound to God, and that God has in some way bound Himself to them. In the humanist's eyes such demands must satisfy the obvious needs of man if they are to be taken seriously. Stripped of their theological sanctions, they must be proved to be conducive to human happiness – or go to the wall. Often it is easy to show that man's interests are best served by obeying God's law, but there are also times when it is not so clear that this is so, and it is on these occasions especially that the God-source of Christian ethics makes a world of difference to the direction moral living can take.

The words 'morals' and 'ethics' in themselves provide useful illustrations of the important difference between God-centred and man-centred thinking. Both are derived from expressions (Latin and Greek) which mean 'custom'. The implication seems to be that we will learn about ethics and morals only as we investigate human habits and customs. We first discover what the 'done thing' is, and then conclude that it 'ought to be done'. For sheer survival in society this amounts to very wise advice, but a sharper contrast with biblical teaching could hardly be found. The Christian is called upon to match his behaviour to *God's* standards, whether they square with contemporary conventions or not. In theological language, he draws his moral convictions from *revelation* (some of which he may not fully understand, especially at first), not from *investigation*.

In the Concordia film *Question 7*, which deals with life in East Berlin, a young Christian who is being victimized for her faith is being entertained to tea by her uncle. He passes her a radish. 'Bite it!' he orders. She does so. 'Look at it now,' he says, 'red on the outside but white on the inside. Why can't you live like that – keeping your Christianity intact on the inside, and conforming to communist standards outwardly?' Patiently she explains that as a Christian she must obey God in her behaviour outwardly, even when His standards conflict with those of society around her. The points of reference are vertical, not horizontal.

In an attempt to escape this conclusion, some have tried to drive a wedge between Jesus' moral teaching and His theology. The Jewish scholar Klausner, for example, writes wistfully, 'The main strength of Jesus lay in his ethical teaching. If we omitted the miracles and a few mystical sayings which tend to deify the Son of Man, and preserved only the moral precepts and parables, the Gospels would count as one of the most wonderful collections of ethical teaching in the world.' But, as Klausner himself admits, this is asking for the impossible. All Jesus' ethical teaching is deeply rooted in His religion. Even the Sermon on the Mount begins with some definitions of happiness which lose all their credibility once the God-language is removed (otherwise how could mourners and the persecuted be called 'happy'?). And Jesus was only following Old Testament precedent in deducing His moral teaching from religious premises. It is no more possible to split away the first four of the Ten Commandments (the religious ones) from the last six, and still remain faithful to the thrust of Old Testament teaching, than to take Jesus' second great commandment ('love your neighbour') and ignore the first ('love your God'). Disentangling religion and morality in the Bible is like trying to unscramble your breakfast egg.

## God's goodness

The New Testament expresses its God-centred approach to morals in two ways.

### 1. The will of God

Twice over in his letter to the Romans Paul equates moral goodness with God's will. 'The will of God', he writes, is 'what is good and acceptable and perfect' – something the Christian discovers when he breaks free from timid conformity to custom and allows his thinking to be reshaped by God's Spirit (Rom. 12: 2). It is those who 'know his will' who 'approve what is excellent' (and not because they strike gold when digging for moral truth by their own effort, but because they are 'instructed in the law' – Rom. 2: 18).

The author of the letter to the Hebrews sounds the same note. His prayer for his readers is that God may 'equip you with everything *good* that you may do *his will*, working in you that which is *pleasing in his sight*' (Heb. 13: 21). And we find Jesus Himself making a similar point in His teaching about God's kingdom. 'Kingdom' in the Gospels usually means 'rule' rather than 'realm'. As the Lord's Prayer makes plain, God's *kingdom* comes when His *will* is done. Or, putting it the other way round, it is those who do the Father's will who 'enter the kingdom' (Mt. 7: 21). And Jesus taught that the moral righteousness needed for entry into the kingdom of heaven is nothing less than full submission to the will of God.

So Christian ethics is basically the conforming of human behaviour to God's will. If a man asks 'What must I do to do good?', the Christian answer is 'Obey God's will'. To live a good moral life means to put oneself under divine orders.

But the Bible goes on to take us one step further.

## 2. The nature of God

Three out of the four Gospels tell us how Jesus met a rich young ruler. According to Mark, the young man began by addressing Jesus as 'Good Teacher'. Jesus immediately took him up on his use of the word 'good'. 'Why do you call me good? *No one is good but God alone*' (Mk. 10: 18). Although this was only a preliminary skirmish before the real battle began, there are two important pieces of information here about the Christian moral standard.

The first thing to pinpoint is Jesus' assumption that *the Christian standard of goodness is personal. God* is good. If we want to discover what goodness is all about, the Bible directs

15

us not to some dusty old textbook on a library shelf, bulging with abstract ethical theories, but to the personal nature of the living God. Unlike any other moral teacher, God is utterly consistent. What He wills, He is. Something is good not just because He commands it as part of His will, but because He exemplifies it as part of His nature.

This is something that comes out very clearly in the Old Testament's account of the way God met with Moses on Mount Sinai. In response to Moses' request, God promised 'I will make all my goodness pass before you, and I will pronounce in your hearing the Name JEHOVAH' (Ex. 33: 19, NEB). Jehovah was the divine name of personal relationship, and the margin of the New English Bible suggests 'character' as an alternative translation for 'goodness'. In other words, God's goodness is the expression of His character, His personality. So when the promise was finally honoured, Moses did not find himself presented with an ethical treatise. He was given instead a revelation of God's character: 'JEHOVAH, the Lord, a god compassionate and gracious, long-suffering, ever constant and true, maintaining constancy to thousands, forgiving iniquity, rebellion, and sin . . . ' (Ex. 34: 6, 7, NEB).

The second point Jesus made in His reply to the young man was that *God's goodness is unique.* 'No one is good but God alone.' And once again this is an idea that has deep roots in the Old Testament. At the very beginning of Israel's life as a nation, God revealed Himself as 'the Holy One'. The word 'holy' contains the idea of moral purity, but its basic meaning is 'different'. The *Holy* God is, by definition, *uniquely* good. So when man asks for a pattern of goodness to follow, the Bible points him to nothing less than the matchless purity of the Holy One Himself. 'Be holy, for I am holy' is a refrain which runs right through the Old Testament, and Jesus takes it up in the Sermon on the Mount: 'You, therefore, must be perfect, as your heavenly Father is perfect' (Mt. 5: 48). Many moralists urge, 'Do what I tell you.' A few would dare to say, 'Do as I do.' But God goes further. He says, 'Be as I am.'

Right at the heart of Christian ethics, then, lies this insistence that progress in moral living comes only through imitating God the Father, the Holy One, and Jesus Christ who is the living demonstration of His moral goodness. 'It was reserved for Christianity', wrote Lecky the historian, 'to present to the world an ideal character, which through all the changes of eighteen centuries has inspired the hearts of men with an impassioned love; has shown itself capable of acting on all ages, nations, temperaments and conditions . . . and has exercised so deep an influence that it may be truly said that the simple record of three short years of active life has done more to regenerate and to soften mankind than all the disquisitions of philosophers, and all the exhortations of moralists.'[1]

## Morality without God?

But this is the point at which the non-Christian moral philosopher enters a strong objection. Making goodness depend on God (assuming he exists) begs all kinds of important questions, he protests. Why *should* man be morally obliged to do his Creator's will? If the answer is 'Because God is good', how can we be so sure? What is the standard of goodness by which God acts? The Christian may reply that to say God conforms to any external moral standard is to strip Him of His deity, but this fails to satisfy a philosopher who does not share Christian presuppositions. The fact that anyone *wills* us to do something is no reason why we *ought* to do it, unless we can be convinced by independent evidence that what he wills is always morally right.

[1] W. E. H. Lecky, *History of European Morals* (Longmans, 1911), quoted by S. B. Babbage in *Sex and Sanity* (Hodder and Stoughton, 1965), p. 92.

To this is added a more practical objection. If moral values are tied too tightly to the authority of God, what will be the result for the nation's morality if what God says no longer goes for the majority of people? Lewis Carroll illustrates the dilemma well in *Alice in Wonderland*. At the end of her stay in Wonderland, Alice successfully defies the terrible Queen of Hearts, tumbling at last to the fact that a pack of cards can do her no harm.

> 'Hold your tongue!' said the Queen, turning purple.
>
> 'I won't,' said Alice.
>
> 'Off with her head!' the Queen shouted at the top of her voice.
>
> Nobody moved.
>
> 'Who cares for you?' said Alice.

Perhaps, like Alice, modern man has outgrown the source of authority which has successfully dictated his behaviour for so long. Even if he only *thinks* he has, the prospect is still alarming. What will we do if the baby of morality vanishes down the plughole along with the bathwater of religion?

Not unnaturally, educationalists worry about this more than most. If moral education is included as part of the school RE syllabus, abandonment of religious belief may result in a frightening indifference to moral values among young people. Some would say it is already happening. Hence the humanists' call for a syllabus of moral education which is completely detached from any religious context. Religion may help a few, but morals are for everyone.

This is powerful pleading, but before we agree that a God-centred approach to morality has nothing to say to non-believers, we need to look again at the curiously wide range of agreement to be found among both Christians and non-Christians on many moral issues. A North London vicar who set out to collect signatures in a campaign to stop morally offensive advertising outside a local cinema was astonished when hundreds of his petition forms came back signed by men and women who never darkened the door of his church. At about the same time, a humanist manifesto was circulating which called for an end to pollution, starvation and social injustice – a cause to which all Christians could give their support. Granted that the sources from which Christians and humanists draw their moral convictions are different (the title of this manifesto is *People First*), and that this difference is important, why is it that Christians and non-Christians so often find themselves, perhaps rather uneasily, standing on the same platform when moral issues are debated?

Part of the answer certainly lies in the area of *common-sense*. Any healthy man has the ability to look at life around him and draw sensible conclusions. He needs no philosophical training to see, for example, that a stable society can exist only if property is respected and people tell the truth to one another. Stealing, vandalism and telling lies are therefore labelled among the 'bad' things it is 'wrong' to do. National law-codes are based on this kind of social reasoning, as are global agreements like the UNO Declaration of Human Rights. Christians subscribe to them, and so do a lot of other people as well.

But this is not all. The common-sense approach to behaviour is supplemented by something else which is not so easy to define. We may call it *moral intuition*. When we are told about a particularly vicious and senseless attack on an old lady, our reaction – if we are charitable – is to say, 'The man must be mad!' We may not be able to explain the way we feel, but we know others will understand. We just 'know' that no human being in his right mind would act as that man has done. This moral sensitivity, which seems to exist quite independently of religious faith, is something politicians are particularly careful to respect. That is no doubt why a government spokesman will always try to justify his policy in moral terms, whether he is speaking to Christians or not. It would be astonishing to hear him say, 'Support me and fight for the triumph of evil over good.' In the same way, both sides in an international dispute take the greatest pains to convince the world that right is on their side.

Although opinions about what is right and what is wrong are expressed in widely differing conventions, there remains this strange phenomenon which C. S. Lewis describes as 'the triumphant monotony of the same indispensable platitudes which meet us in culture after culture'. Moral sensitivity is not the private prerogative of the Christian. Everywhere we are met by a tacit admission that there are basic moral distinctions which can be drawn, and which must be defended. If, therefore, the Christian who obeys God's will and the non-Christian who follows social common-sense and his moral intuition both arrive at the same conclusions on a great many important issues, why not drop all reference to God, as the humanist asks, and work for a common morality?

## Morals and the Creator

Here it is the Christian's turn to dig in his heels. Not all men are Christians. But all men are created, *and all men have a natural moral sense because they bear the image of their Creator*. This is the Christian position. God's net is thrown over the whole of human moral sensitivity. Non-Christians and those who have never read the Ten Commandments, writes Paul, have the moral requirements of the Ten Commandments 'written on their hearts'. In contemporary language, the non-Christian who signs a petition against pornography and the humanist who calls for an end to social injustice are both acknowledging the inbuilt moral law of the God in whom they do not believe.

This is a bold claim, but one that is basic to the Christian understanding of morality. A Christian may agree that it is sometimes good practical politics to argue for a particular moral standard, like sexual fidelity in marriage, without mentioning the word 'God', but when people respond to such a call he insists that they are responding to their Creator, whether they realize it or not. In his letter to the Ephesians we find Paul defending truth-telling and opposing stealing in an apparently non-theological way. 'Let everyone speak the truth with his neighbour,' he writes, 'for we are members one of another.' Because telling lies destroys the confidence one member of the community ought to have in another, people should tell the truth. In a similar way, Paul goes on, because a healthy society thrives on giving and not on greed, 'Let the thief no longer steal, but rather let him labour, doing honest work with his hands, so that he may be able to give to those in need.' These are arguments which ought to make an instant appeal to any socially-minded citizen, Christian or not, and Paul refrains from drawing in God-sanctions to give his case a boost. But in the sentence which introduces this section he makes it quite clear that these moral demands which sound so acceptable in their own right are in fact well-founded on the revealed will of the Creator. When Christians display a social conscience they are in fact showing evidence of their new nature which is *created after the likeness of God* in true righteousness and holiness' (Eph. 4: 24–28).

There is one further factor, which points the Christian to his need for the special revelation which only God can give. As well as teaching that man's moral sense derives from his creation in the image of God, the Bible also makes it plain that this creation-image has been spoiled by sin. Trying to make accurate moral judgments by the light of human moral sense alone is like attempting to read road-signs through a misted-up windscreen. Even the larger lettering may be mis-read or missed entirely. And the problem of finding the right route is only one aspect of man's total moral dilemma as he travels through life. With strange perversity, human nature urges him to ignore the sign-posts God puts in his way, even when he can see their message clearly. In pre-motorway days Calvin compared the man who goes through life relying only on the guidance of his innate moral sense to a traveller walking along a path on a pitch-black night in the middle of a thunderstorm, with only the light of an occasional flash of lightning to give him his bearings. To blunder through life in that way is an open invitation to disaster, especially if the scanty guidance that *is* available is ignored.

Because of sin, man needs something to clear his moral vision, and this is exactly the function revelation performs. If we may stretch the windscreen analogy a little, God has provided us with a 'demister' in the shape of His revealed moral truth. When we read the Bible, and especially when we meet with Jesus Christ, we are given a clearer sight of our Creator's character, and a fuller knowledge of His will. In a vague and unsatisfactory way, the knowledge was there before, but God's special revelation clears our vision. We must deal in a later chapter with the equally pressing problem of how to turn moral knowledge into action.

It is interesting to notice how some honest thinkers who stop short of full Christian commitment still recognize in Jesus' teaching the crystallization of their own moral aspirations. 'Nor even now', admits John Stuart Mill, 'would it be easy, even for an unbeliever, to find a better translation of the rule of virtue from the abstract into the concrete than to endeavour so to live that Christ would approve our life.' Bernard Shaw says much the same thing rather more vividly in the Preface to *Androcles and the Lion*: 'We have always had a curious feeling that though we crucified Christ on a stick, He somehow managed to get hold of the right end of it, and that, if we were better men, we might try His plan.' The moral attraction of revelation is strong, even for those who do not accept it as such.

Turning to the Bible after reading a textbook of moral philosophy is not a comfortable experience. It is rather like leaving a snug fireside to face a storm of sleet without a raincoat. We find very little ethical reasoning in Scripture to stimulate cosy discussion. A moral philosopher must back his statements with solid arguments if he is to escape ridicule, but the Creator has no need to give reasons for what He demands. So instead of arguments, suggestions and advice we meet commands and prohibitions in God's revelation – no less in the teaching of Jesus than in the sternest parts of the Old Testament. The Bible does not aim to be philosophically conclusive. It does claim to be right.

Here then is the right starting-point for any discussion of the Christian approach to morality. The moral standard is the character of God. We understand more about goodness as we learn more about Him. To know His will clearly we need the light of special revelation, but all men, by virtue of their creation, have His moral law 'written on their hearts'. If they try to argue its influence away, and follow a different code, they are automatically in the wrong. God's will is not one option among many.

# OBEYING IN LOVE

For some readers, the final paragraphs of the last chapter may have struck a jarring note. We live in a world that is in revolt against authoritarianism in any shape or form. When fewer and fewer people around us are prepared to do what they are told without adequate explanation, however exalted the source of authority from which the orders come, it does seem rather incongruous to go on writing about a God who demands unquestioning obedience to His will.

Nowadays the critical attitude to authority begins in the classroom. Because it is an important part of modern educational theory to encourage enquiring minds, and to investigate and challenge all accepted opinions, any set of traditional moral values is automatically at risk. Strong, independent arguments must be brought in to reinforce moral codes or their authority, however long-established, will count for nothing. The very first aim of education, we are told, is to prepare young people for adulthood, and any adult should be equipped to make up his own mind about moral matters, without the safety-net of authority to catch him if he takes a false step.

Some modern theologians, catching the spirit of the age, would go even further than this. They point out that God made man with a capacity for moral choice. If we try to deprive healthy men and women of their right to choose what they ought or ought not to do, we are posing a direct threat to their human dignity. To coerce people into slavish obedience to some moral 'rule of life' is to treat them not only as sub-*adult* but as sub-*human*. And to attempt this kind of thing in God's name is to misunderstand His purpose for humanity entirely. He never intended man to become some kind of ethical robot, programmed to be a slave forever to a long list of moral 'do's and don'ts'.

## Rules – out!

It is no surprise, then, to find Christian advocates of the so-called New Morality, such as John Robinson of *Honest to God* fame and the American Joseph Fletcher, right out in the forefront of the assault on all systems of ethics in which – to use Fletcher's words – 'solutions are preset, and you can "look them up" in a book, a Bible or a confessor's manual'. Their case against any approach to morality that relies on rule-keeping as its mainstay can be reduced to two main criticisms, both of which deserve our attention.

The first serious charge is that *living by rules is unsatisfactory*.

We may applaud the man who buys his wife a box of chocolates on their wedding anniversary, but if we find out afterwards that he visited the confectioners only out of a sense of husbandly duty, our admiration for his thoughtfulness is soured. Even the most apparently 'loving' action leaves a nasty taste in the mouth once we suspect that it has come straight out of some private list of the right-things-to-do. Every minister, for example, knows that one or two of his regulars are in church Sunday by Sunday mainly because they think it is their duty to be there. He is glad they come, no doubt, but how much more thrilled he would be if one day their cold sense of obligation warmed into a real desire to worship! No-one has to be told that wooden obedience to a set of rules is a very poor substitute for behaviour which springs from genuine heartfelt conviction.

25

The second, and more weighty, criticism levelled at law-morality is that *living by rules can be positively harmful*.

To underline this, Joseph Fletcher, in his controversial book *Situation Ethics*, tells about two incidents on the great trail westward across North America in the eighteenth century. On one occasion a Scottish woman saw that her small baby, ill and crying, was betraying the whole of her group to the Indians. But she clung to her child, and they were all caught and killed. The second incident was almost a carbon-copy of the first, but had a different outcome. A Negro mother, seeing how her crying child was endangering another trail party, killed it with her own hands. As a result they were able to travel silently and so reach the safety of a nearby fort. 'Which woman', asks Fletcher, 'made the right decision?' For him, the answer is obvious. The first mother lived by the rule-book. She would not commit infanticide. The second, for the sake of everyone around her, set aside both her motherly instincts and the commandment 'Thou shalt not kill'. Through the sacrifice of her baby it is she who has earned the praise of the history-books, and rightly so.

In a less dramatic way (but perhaps all the more telling for that), the Gospels illustrate the perils of a moral life which is totally dominated by rules and regulations. Jesus' repeated confrontations with the Pharisees highlight the inadequacy and the danger of living in slavery to the rule-book. Mark tells of one typical incident when Jesus met a man with a withered hand in the synagogue. The Pharisees watched eagerly, but not out of any compassion for the sick man. Their interest lay solely in the preservation of their intricate network of Sabbath regulations, not in the healing of a human being. They watched Jesus, 'to see whether he would heal him on the sabbath, so that they might accuse him' (Mk. 3: 2). Determination to maintain their prestige as champion rule-keepers had depersonalized their moral attitudes, and made them callous under the pretext of piety.

Their devotion to the law had effectively insulated them against the love of God. In Mark Twain's vivid phrase, they were 'good men in the worst sense of the word'.

## Love – in!

It was in sharp distinction to rigid Pharisaic legalism, say the exponents of the 'New Morality', that Jesus stressed the primacy of love. *Love puts the needs of people first.* 'Nothing in the world', Fletcher writes, 'causes so much conflict of conscience as the continual, conventional payment of lip-service to moral "laws" that are constantly flouted in practice because they are too rigid to fit the facts of life. Many people prefer to fit reality to rules than to fit rules to reality.' So it is that we find Jesus showing far more concern for a law-breaker like the woman taken in adultery, than for the law she had broken. Love always puts people before principles.

Again, while law strait-jackets its victims with pre-fabricated decisions, the way of *love allows for the flexibility which different situations demand.* The individual must be given freedom to choose the most loving course of action for himself, without any overriding obligations to an inflexible code of rules imposed upon him from above. And, unlike the rule-book, love offers no shelter for the calculating person who is content to do his duty but no more. When Peter asked Jesus how many times he was required to forgive an enemy, he was displaying the law-man's attitude to behaviour. Jesus' reply ('till seventy times seven') banished moral arithmetic from the scene once and for all (unless we believe Peter was meant to count up to 490!). There are no ceilings to the obligations of love. The driver who sees a wheel wobbling loose on the car in front, and merely slows down to avoid being involved in a pile-up, is doing nothing against the law, but love is not thereby satisfied. Rule-keeping panders to minimum standards, but love requires something over and above a 'mind your own business' approach to morality.

Above all, Fletcher argues, if we read the Bible carefully, we discover that in Christian teaching *love replaces law.* Paul in particular is quite clear about this. 'Now we are discharged from the law, dead to that which held us captive, so that we serve not under the old written code but in the new life of the Spirit. . . . For Christ is the end of the law. . . . He who loves his neighbour has fulfilled the law. The commandments, "You shall not commit adultery, You shall not kill, You shall not steal, You shall not covet," and any other commandment, are summed up in this sentence, "You shall love your neighbour as yourself" ' (Rom. 7: 6; 10: 4; 13: 8, 9).

The last sentence faithfully reflects Jesus' teaching too. 'Teacher,' asked a lawyer, 'which is the great commandment in the law?' And Jesus replied with His famous love-summary of the Ten Commandments. 'You shall love the Lord your God with all your heart, and with all your soul, and with all your mind. This is the great and first commandment. And a second is like it, You shall love your neighbour as yourself. On these two commandments depend all the law and the prophets' (Mt. 22: 35–40).

Fletcher and Robinson conclude that, although moral rules have a helpful advisory role, love must reign supreme as the sole director of Christian conduct. It is no good pretending that we can serve both love and law at the same time, because we can all think of occasions when they pull us in different directions. If conflict comes, as it surely will, we must be in no doubt as to which of the two we should follow. All rules are 'love's servants and subordinates, to be quickly kicked out of the house if they forget their place and try to take over' (*Situation Ethics*, p. 78). Living by love is undeniably more difficult than living by law, but 'the fact that the old landmarks are disappearing is not something simply to be deplored. If we have the courage, it is something to be welcomed – as a challenge to Christian ethics to shake itself loose from the supports of supernaturalistic legalism' (*Honest to God*, p. 117).


## Love and obedience

There is so much that is fresh and attractive in this presentation, especially the strong insistence on the supremacy of love, which seems admirably to match the main thrust of the New Testament's moral teaching. We all know, and secretly abhor, the grim-faced paragon of virtue who strides through life festooned with ribbons of ethical red tape, the moral rule-book poking ostentatiously out of his pocket. Jesus, we are convinced, was never like that.

And yet, when the records of Jesus' teaching are examined more carefully, it soon becomes apparent that He did not simply replace moral rules by the criterion of love. On some occasions he spoke very warmly about the Old Testament law. 'Think not', He said, 'that I have come to abolish the law and the prophets; I have come not to *abolish* them but to *fulfil* them. . . . Whoever then relaxes one of the least of these commandments and teaches men so, shall be called least in the kingdom of heaven' (Mt. 5: 17, 19).

There is no hint here that Christians are meant to choose between obeying the commandments and following the way of love, as though these are optional alternatives. To make matters even more plain, 'obey' is a word we quite frequently find on Jesus' lips when He is setting out His own moral teaching. Once, speaking in a context of love, He stated quite bluntly, 'He who does not *obey* the Son shall not see life' (Jn. 3: 36). If men set out to follow Jesus, allowing their lives to be dominated by His love, they are not thereby putting themselves beyond the reach of any moral rules.

Paul's teaching follows Jesus' closely, though it is complicated by his different uses of the word 'law'. Quite often in the Epistles 'law' is no more than a shorthand abbreviation for 'law-keeping as a means of earning God's approval', and in this sense the rule of law certainly has no place in the Christian life. According to the gospel, justification before God comes through faith, not by keeping rules, so that in Paul's words 'Christ is the *end of the law*, that every one who has *faith* may be *justified*' (Rom. 10: 4).

But sometimes Paul means by 'law' the expression of God's will. 'The law is holy,' he reminds Christians at Rome (Rom. 7: 12), 'and the commandment is holy and just and good' – just like God, in fact, which is only what we should expect if our conclusion in chapter 1 (that God's will is the expression of His character) is valid. In this sense, there is no question at all about the law being obsolete for Christians. The German scholar Rudolf Bultmann summarizes Paul's double-edged law teaching very well: 'Christianity is the end of the law so far as it claimed to be the way to salvation,' he writes. 'So far as it contains God's demand, it retains its validity.'

Paul's approach to the keeping of God's law, then, dovetails with the teaching of Christ. 'Love is the fulfilling of the law' (Rom. 13: 10) not because it supersedes any need to keep God's rules, but because it provides the fullest description of His moral law's true meaning. When men have been justified by faith, right is still right and wrong is still wrong, and the will of God still finds expression in the formulae of His law. Keeping moral rules and doing the loving thing do not seem to be nearly so opposed in New Testament teaching as writers like Robinson and Fletcher would have us believe. It is hard, really, to see how they possibly could be. If the revealed law of Scripture expresses the will of God, and 'love' is the best one-word description of His character, any effort to oppose the two must represent an attempt to split the divine personality.

## Delighting in law

So far, however, we have only been clearing the ground. If the proper New Testament formula is not 'love *or* law' but 'love *in* and *through* law', how are we to mix these two essential ingredients in our practical moral living? Is it possible to keep the warmth and spontaneity of love, and at the same time obey a set of moral principles?

To find out the answer, we must turn first to the Old Testament. The days are fortunately gone when respected scholars contrasted the dark ages of life under Old Testament law with the new era of grace and freedom heralded by the coming of Christ. It was sometimes forgotten that Jesus took both His great love commandments straight out of the pages of Leviticus and Deuteronomy. Love and grace were prominent features of the old covenant, just as there is an important place for law (as we have seen) under the new. But perhaps, even now, not enough attention is paid to the very remarkable *attitude to law-keeping* that is displayed by some Old Testament writers.

These short excerpts from one of the Psalms are typical: 'Lead me in the path of thy commandments, for I delight in it. Incline my heart to thy testimonies, and not to gain! . . . for I find my delight in thy commandments, which I love. . . . The law of thy mouth is better to me than thousands of gold and silver pieces' (Ps. 119: 35, 36, 47, 72).

Allowing for poetic imagery, if that expression of devotion to the law does not surprise us by its fervour, we ought perhaps to try translating it into the contemporary terms of a law-keeping we understand better. 'Lead me in the way of the Income-Tax law,' we might begin, 'for I delight in it. Incline my heart to the small print, and not to personal gain. The pronouncements of Her Majesty's Inspector of Taxes are better to me than thousands of gold and silver pieces!'

Comparing God's law and state legislation is of course unfair (though in Bible times people saw a definite link between the two), but at once we find ourselves in a different world. It did not seem incongruous to the Psalmist to sing about his love for a set of rules. Today it is hard to imagine even the most enthusiastic Government commissioning the Poet Laureate to compose an ode in honour of the statute book! When theologians like Fletcher and Robinson write about 'law' and 'rules' they assume – almost as a matter of definition – that rule-keeping is something dull, dry and oppressive in itself. The law's main function is to stop us doing what we want to do, and we long to be released from its restrictions. The writers of the Old Testament did not see God's law in that light at all.

The vital difference lies in the area of *relationships*. In all probability, I enjoy no kind of relationship with the tax inspector. The exercise of his lawful authority is therefore cold and distant as far as I am concerned. The 'he' who sends the printed letters might as well be an 'it' – and in the days of computerization that may be nearer the truth than I imagine. When I break his regulations it does not occur to me that I have personally wounded the tax-man himself, and I am fairly sure he does not feel that way about me either. There is no personal relationship between the two of us to be strained or broken.

All this is utterly foreign to the spirit of the Bible. In the Old Testament, God's law is securely founded on the personal covenant relationship He has already established with His people. That is why the Ten Commandments are couched in the familiar second person ('*Thou* shalt not . . .'), instead of the more remote third person ('*It* is forbidden . . .') which is so much more popular with modern legislators. God's rules reflect His own loving character which He longs for His people to share, and because they love Him, and want that relationship deepened, they obey His law out of a full heart and not in a spirit of grudging reluctance. Were they to be relieved of the law's demands, it could only mean that God intended to withdraw His offer to enter into relationship with them. And that would be disastrous.

When we step across to the New Testament, we find many echoes of this theme. 'All who *keep his commandments*', writes John, '*abide in him*, and he in them.' Keeping God's law enhances our relationship with Him – and the opposite is equally true. 'He who says "*I know him*" but *disobeys his commandments* is a liar, and the truth is not in him' (1 Jn. 3: 24; 2: 4).

In his book *No New Morality*, Douglas Rhymes complains that 'society has the wrong visual image of Christian morality . . . because it has often been presented as a rule rather than a relationship'. There is more than a grain of truth in that, but we shall find ourselves in an equally false position if, in the name of Christianity, we lay all the stress on relationships and play down rules. According to both New and Old Testaments a genuine relationship cannot exist without any rules, not at least this side of the grave.

It is quite wrong, then, to assume that there must be an inevitable clash between obeying rules and living in relationship. We know from our own human experience that the deeper a love-relationship becomes, the more willingly one partner will do what the other wishes without having to ask questions. Demanding all the answers first is a sign that the element of trust, which is necessary to cement any relationship, is as yet missing. Without apparently any embarrassment at all, Jesus described the perfect love-relationship He enjoyed with His Father in terms of full obedience, and He held up the same love/obedience pattern to His disciples as the ideal they should all strive to achieve. 'If you keep my commandments, you will abide in my love,' He said, 'just as I have kept my Father's commandments and abide in his love' (Jn. 15: 10).

## The burden of law

A few sentences later, Jesus drove the same point home by spelling out the responsibilities of friendship. 'You are my friends', He told them, '*if you do what I command you.*' But in calling them 'friends', He made an important distinction. 'No longer do I call you *slaves*,' He said, 'for the slave does not know what his master is doing; but I have called you friends' (Jn. 15: 14, 15 mg.). Both friends and slaves are called to obey, but they do so for quite distinct reasons. The slave conforms because he *has* to; the friend because he *wants* to.

It is here that the New Morality's complaints make a great deal of sense. The *friend* enjoys a close relationship with the master which makes his will an object of desire. As John puts it, 'this is the love of God, that we keep his commandments. And his commandments are not burdensome' (1 Jn. 5: 3). But the *slave* has no relationship of that sort to make obedience attractive. To him, having to obey orders is an irksome restriction, a heavy burden to bear.

Life provides plenty of evidence to show how oppressive law can become when relationships break down. The workings of the Industrial Relations Act in Great Britain are a fine example. Both sides of industry acknowledge that a good relationship cannot be imposed by law (any more than a couple can be ordered to fall in love), and some would claim that any so-called solution forced upon conflicting parties by a law-court does more harm than good. The set of rules for fair industrial practice on which the court bases its decision may not be bad. What really rankles with one side or the other is that a third party is empowered to coerce them into 'peace'.

Everyone agrees that the ideal answer would be for management and shop-floor to get together and draw up a list of working principles by which disputes could be settled amicably 'within the family'. The working principles might be identical with the legally-imposed set of rules, but all would recognize the important difference between an agreement settled within a healthy relationship and a law imposed forcibly from the outside. In some countries (notably Japan) industry works more smoothly, not because there are fewer rules and regulations, but because the personal bond of trust between employer and employee is still holding. Rules within a good working relationship are not burdensome.

This is the point the New Testament makes in its assessment of man's attitude to God's law. Basically it is the same distinction as the one Jesus drew between the friend and the slave. If no close relationship exists between the individual and God, any requirement to obey His will is an intolerable imposition, and the fact that the Creator has a sovereign right to impose His wishes makes matters worse, not better. It is only when the broken relationship is mended, when the unwilling slave becomes a friend (or, in Paul's terminology, a son) that God's moral law becomes a delight instead of an irritant. The rules themselves do not change (because God's will does not alter), but the attitude of the individual towards them undergoes a radical transformation. The old oppressive commandments which unbearably stifled freedom of moral expression in the past suddenly become 'the perfect law . . . of liberty' (Jas. 1 : 25). The Christian, now intimately related to God by faith, exchanges 'the law of sin and death' for 'the law of the Spirit of life in Christ Jesus' (Rom. 8: 2). Love brings to law a new warmth, and law provides love with sturdy backbone.


## The profit of law

Leaving aside for the moment the very important function *state* law has in protecting society at large from those who would injure it, we are now in a position to summarize the two main positive roles God's law can play in the believer's life.

First of all, *the law provides moral information*. In the measured words of Calvin's *Institutes*, Christians need the moral law of the Bible as 'the best instrument for enabling them daily to learn with greater truth and certainty what the will of the Lord is which they aspire to follow, and to confirm them in this knowledge'.

Some would say that this function of law is now redundant as far as the Christian is concerned, granted the will to love. In *Honest to God*, for example, John Robinson argues that 'love alone, because, as it were, it has a built-in moral compass, enabling it to "home" intuitively upon the deepest need of the other, can allow itself to be directed completely by the situation'. Human nature suggests otherwise, however. Love's moral compass is a delicate instrument, and its homing device can very easily be jammed by sentimentality and self-deception. Joseph Fletcher, who stands shoulder to shoulder with Robinson on this issue, admits that people will make many moral mistakes as they try to discover the way of love in different situations. He looks forward to the day when some of the errors can be eliminated by the use of a computer which will help men to do their love calculations more accurately. (The computer suggestion comes a little strangely from a writer who insists that 'the Christian conscience is not a vending machine, with handles to pull and prepackaged answers to spew out of a slot'.)

The Bible's answer is that love's moral compass is neither the individual's private intuition nor some kind of ethical 'Ernie', but the revealed moral law of God as it is interpreted and applied by the Holy Spirit. 'Through the law comes knowledge of sin' (Rom. 3: 20). This is no doubt why the ethical sections of the New Testament Epistles are full of direct or indirect references to the Ten Commandments.

Paul certainly did not regard it as adequate moral instruction merely to say to his converts 'Love and do what you like'. He felt it necessary to spell out what love meant in the simplest practical terms. 'Let everyone speak the truth. . . . Let the thief no longer steal. . . . Let no evil talk come out of your mouths. . . . Be kind to one another. . . . Do not get drunk. . . . Honour your father and mother.' Perhaps when some people ask to be told what to do in particular situations, rather than work out moral problems for themselves, they are being more realistic than lazy.

Humour often provides the best illustrations. A cartoon appeared some time ago in *Christianity Today* showing Moses holding the two stone tablets of the Ten Commandments and looking out with anger over the people of Israel as they worshipped the golden calf Aaron had made. An eager young man is saying to Moses, 'Aaron said perhaps you'd let us reduce them to "Act responsibly in love" ' (quoted, to his credit, by Joseph Fletcher in *Situation Ethics*).

The second important function law has to play in the moral life is *to stimulate the conscience*. In his letter to the Galatians, Paul describes the law as 'our custodian until Christ came' (Gal. 3: 24). The custodian's task in Bible times was not to act as a schoolmaster, as the Authorized Version suggests (so that the law makes a man good up to a point, from which Christ takes over to 'finish' him). His role was to discipline and deliver the child to the teacher. The law fulfils this function when it witnesses to God's ideal moral standards, and so prevents men from becoming satisfied with anything less. In achieving this, it also has a distressing side-effect. If something is forbidden, doing it immediately becomes more attractive (as the homosexual Westermarck knew who, in the old days, 'would be very sorry to see the English law changed, as the practice would then lose its charm'). If there is a notice saying 'No Entry', we automatically want to see what is on the other side of the door. If a book is banned, its circulation soars.

On both counts, then, law the custodian does not let us rest until it has led us to Christ to find forgiveness and strength. It exposes our impotence to live a life that squares with God's standards, and it stimulates our desire to sin even more than we otherwise would. As Paul discovered for himself, taking just the last of the Ten Commandments, 'I should never have felt guilty of the sin of coveting if I had not heard the Law saying "Thou shalt not covet". But the sin in me, finding in the commandment an opportunity to express itself, stimulated all my covetous desires' (Rom. 7: 7, 8, Phillips).

And law's task does not end when it has delivered its charge to Christ because, although the redeemed Christian finds release from bondage to sin (so that temptation is no longer irresistible), his need for discipline is as great as ever. There is no such thing as instant sanctification, nor do non-Christians have a monopoly of moral complacency. The law is the Holy Spirit's spur to goad the Christian conscience to a more and more realistic discipleship until, in Spurgeon's words, 'it should shiver when even the ghost of a sin goes by'.

Let us sum up. There is no clash between obeying God's law and living in His love. On the contrary, our desire to keep His law is a sure sign that our love-relationship with Him is in a healthy state. By respecting His rules, we learn more about His will and find the stimulus to live a life which approximates more closely to His standard of perfection.

John Wesley was being absolutely faithful to the gospel of grace and freedom he preached when he exclaimed, 'I cannot spare the law one moment, no more than I can spare Christ; seeing I now want it as much, to keep me to Christ, as ever I wanted it to bring me to Him. . . . Indeed, each is continually sending me to the other, the law to Christ, and Christ to the law.'

# STICKS AND CARROTS

Jesus respected and reinforced the moral law of the Old Testament, and when He saw fit to amplify it He did not hesitate to demand the same kind of obedience for His own teaching as was traditionally shown to the commandments of the law. So much is clear from the New Testament. Very rarely in the Gospels do we find Jesus giving advice or making suggestions, as a modern moralist might. Not once did He so much as hint to His disciples that when they followed Him they could cut loose from the old moral rules and lead a life of 'free love'. And there was a ringing note of authority in His own teaching which made ordinary people sit up and take notice whenever He spoke out on moral issues.

Nevertheless, if we see Jesus *simply* as a moral law-teacher with popular appeal, our picture of Him will be a distorted one. The scribes and Pharisees were the law-teachers *par excellence* in New Testament times, yet Jesus made it quite clear that the moral demands He was making were far more radical than any of the precepts of their established law-codes. In the Sermon on the Mount, for example, immediately after a clear, 'safe' policy statement upholding the authority of the Old Testament law ('Whoever then relaxes one of the least of these commandments and teaches men so, shall be called least in the kingdom of heaven'), He went on to say something which must have shocked and embarrassed many of His listeners. 'For I tell you, unless your righteousness *exceeds* that of the scribes and Pharisees, you will never enter the kingdom of heaven' (Mt. 5: 19, 20).

## Attitudes and motives

In the rest of the Sermon on the Mount, Jesus draws on a fund of illustrations to make His meaning clear. The Ten Commandments forbade adultery. So does Jesus. But what about those thoughts that pass through Mr A's mind as he watches his next-door neighbour's pretty wife and mentally undresses her in the privacy of his bedroom? He would never actually commit adultery with her, any more than he would dare to murder Mr B who treats her so badly – but the murderous thoughts are there in his mind all the same, along with the lust.

Jesus taught that a man's thought-life is as important, morally, as his outward conduct. The man who is consumed with hatred for somebody else is morally at risk, even though he is held back by fear of the law from committing an act of murder. He may do no more than look lustfully at another man's wife, but in doing just that he 'has already committed adultery with her in his heart' (Mt. 5: 28).

In tracing problems of conduct right back to their source in the mind and heart, Jesus is penetrating to an area of moral sensitivity which no code of civil law can touch. The law of the land can prescribe or forbid only certain words or actions which can afterwards be checked by observation. It cannot legislate for the inner attitudes from which those words and actions spring. It may be possible to outlaw racial *discrimination*, but the racial *prejudice* of the landlord who finds he has no vacancies when the student on the doorstep has a black face, is beyond the power of any law to control. Discrimination is an outward act, prejudice an inner attitude. The one is within the reach of the law, but the other is not. No doubt it is right for a country to have a

Race Relations Act to define how people ought to behave and to check the worst racist outrages, but it would be living in a fool's paradise to presume that, once this has been done, the underlying prejudices will automatically disappear. Law is impotent to change character and disposition.

In this respect, Jesus was not a moral law-man in the orthodox sense. The main question He asked of anyone was not 'Do you lead a law-abiding life?', but 'What kind of *person* ought you to be?' He had surprisingly little to say about crime or even the 'sins of the flesh'. Paul is far more explicit than Jesus about sexual sin, for example. On the two outstanding occasions when cases of sexual irregularity were brought to Jesus (at Simon the Pharisee's house, and in the temple when He was presented with the test case of a woman caught red-handed in adultery), He did not storm at the culprits but deliberately steered the conversation round to confound the critics and the hypocritical motives which lay behind their expressions of moral indignation.

His positive moral teaching, too, reveals the same emphasis on inward attitudes and motives. The Sermon on the Mount, which most would recognize as the peak of Jesus' ethical teaching, opens with the nine Beatitudes (or the 'Beautiful Attitudes' as they have appropriately been nicknamed), which are not really rules for conduct at all, but a list of God's congratulations to those who display certain *attitudes* to life – the 'poor in *spirit*' and the 'pure *in heart*'.

Jesus, then, taught that inner attitudes are all-important. Even the best activities, like praying and giving to a good cause, are spoiled if they are inspired by wrong motives. And, as usual, the other New Testament writers follow Jesus' lead. It is in this spirit that Paul, when he encourages the Christians at Ephesus to 'speak the truth', is careful to add the vital motive which must characterize all Christian truth-telling. Do it, he says, 'in love' (Eph. 4: 15). There is a great difference, morally, between telling somebody a

41

home-truth in a spirit of maliciousness and half-concealed glee, and saying exactly the same thing out of genuine compassion. The difference lies in motivation, and in Christian ethics motives matter enormously.

Christians, of course, are not the only people to stress the importance of motives. Advertisers, for example, gain their living by stimulating the hidden desires which (they hope) will prompt us to buy their products. By a sharp tug on one end of the chain they hope to ring a bell at the other, and the booming state of the advertising industry shows that their efforts are not in vain. Once harness the motivating force of a man's desires, and his conduct can be predicted with a fair degree of accuracy. It is no more than a commonplace of life, in fact, to provide people with inducements and deterrents which will encourage them to conform to particular behaviour patterns. The old 'carrot and stick' principle which makes a donkey move is still the one parents and teachers use (in a more or less refined way) when they reward and punish children. And there is nothing necessarily 'immoral' about this. If it is right to have laws which direct men's behaviour for good social ends, it cannot be wrong to influence the thinking which lies behind their actions. The process of character building only becomes morally offensive when, as with brain-washing and certain extreme forms of advertising technique, a deliberate attempt is made to erode the individual's freedom to make final moral choices for himself.

It is hardly surprising, therefore, to find so much attention paid in the Bible to the powerful influences which motivate men's conduct. The Creator is not to be satisfied with conduct that merely conforms to the external standards of society's law-codes, 'for the Lord sees not as man sees; man looks on the outward appearance, but the Lord looks on the heart' (1 Sa. 16: 7). Jesus makes much the same point in His 'treasure' illustrations. 'Where your treasure is,' He taught, 'there will your heart be also.' 'How can you

42

speak good, when you are evil? For out of the abundance of the heart the mouth speaks. The good man out of his good treasure brings forth good, and the evil man out of his evil treasure brings forth evil' (Lk. 12: 34; Mt. 12: 34, 35). God wants *consistent* Christians, men and women whose inner motives are consistent with their outward actions.

## Rewards and punishments

What does surprise and shock many people, however, is the apparently *selfish* desires which the Bible stimulates in its attempts to get men to lead a God-centred life. We are told that the Christian life should be one of selfless service, yet the incentives God gives men to live in this way seem to appeal rather blatantly to human self-interest. Otherwise, how are we to interpret those Bible verses which entice us to obey God by the promise of rewards in heaven, or deter us from disobedience by threats of punishment in hell? One contemporary writer, noting that few modern preachers now speak about heaven and hell, comments: 'The reason is not that they have ceased to believe heaven and hell are in some sense real, but that they feel that such appeals are unworthy, and ethically defective.'[1]

Whatever the reasons for the silence from the pulpits, it is impossible to eliminate this strain of doctrine from the New Testament, and significantly the theme of heaven and hell is one that is particularly prominent in Jesus' own teaching. The last of the nine Beatitudes, for instance, finishes with a word of encouragement to Christians who are suffering persecution – 'Rejoice and be glad, *for your reward is great in heaven*' (Mt. 5: 12); and this is balanced a little later by a word of warning in a similar context – 'Do not fear those who kill the body but cannot kill the soul; *rather fear him*

[1] L. H. Marshall, *The Challenge of New Testament Ethics* (Macmillan, 1966), p. 203.

*who can destroy both soul and body in hell*' (Mt. 10: 28). Further on in Matthew's Gospel, Jesus' advice to those who want to be '*greatest in the kingdom of heaven*' is closely followed by severe warnings about careless attitudes to sin – 'it is better for you to enter life maimed or lame than with two hands or two feet *to be thrown into the eternal fire*' (Mt. 18: 4, 8). And these examples are typical of many others which could just as easily be cited.

It is naive to pretend that sayings like these will not exercise a powerful influence on human motivation, however much we would prefer to think otherwise. Many today would sympathize with the proverbial old woman of Alexandria who is said to have walked the city streets with a jug of water in one hand and a flaming torch in the other, declaring that she wanted to put out the fires of hell and destroy heaven, so that men might love God for Himself alone. But the fact remains that many people today are first attracted to Christ (as people always have been) for frankly *selfish* reasons, in a desire to gain for themselves the benefits of eternal life, or to avoid punishment for sin.

There are three things to be said about such appeals to self-interest, which may throw some light on the Bible's approach to rewards and punishments and to motivation in general.

### *1. Biblical teaching is realistic*

It so happened that two young men in trouble with the police arrived on the minister's doorstep independently on the same evening. One of them had come with an entry form for the army which he wanted the minister to countersign. It was made out in his brother's name, because he himself had been discharged from the service with ignominy some time previously for selling his rifle. In a flash of inspiration, the minister turned to the second man and asked his advice. 'You shouldn't sign it, sir,' he said. 'Why not?' asked the minister, greatly relieved. 'Because he's bound to get found out,' came the reply.

It was not the best answer (or the one the minister would have given), but at least it was realistic. On that occasion any talk of 'dishonesty' would have fallen on deaf ears. It would be very nice to think that no man would ever again defraud, assault or steal from anyone else if a compulsory course of training in social responsibility were to be built into the state's educational system, but realism warns us that it would be courting disaster to remove all deterrents of the penal code on those grounds alone. Human nature being what it is, a law without teeth would soon be disregarded. Adequate deterrents will always be needed to restrain anti-social conduct. Some would go further and say that, as well as punishing crime, society should be providing more in the way of positive practical inducements to foster *pro*-social behaviour. The birth-control lobby, for example, would be glad to see much more financial encouragement given to small families to remain that way. Obviously any developments in this direction would have to be carefully watched in case basic personal liberties are infringed, but the principle can hardly be attacked on moral grounds if the idea of social deterrents is accepted. Reward is only the other side of the punishment coin.

Many people, however, while accepting the need for deterrents and inducements at the social level, are far less happy when the same principles are carried over into the private sector of spiritual and moral life. They see the necessity for keeping rigorous penalties to deter crime, but the idea of a God who holds threats of punishment over men's heads for sin seems distastefully sub-Christian. But in the Gospels we find that Jesus Himself did not hesitate to use such appeals. He saw human nature through the eyes of a realist. As John tells his readers, He 'needed no one to bear witness of man; for he himself knew what was in man' (Jn. 2: 25). And He declined to address sinners as though they were saints. All the people Jesus met in the course of His ministry were either totally dominated, or at least partly influenced, by considerations of self-interest, and He spoke to them as they were, not as He would have liked them to be. One suspects that He would not necessarily want to change His approach if He found Himself addressing a modern congregation – even if in the hymn before the sermon everyone had sung with apparent sincerity,

> 'My God, I love Thee; not because
> I hope for heaven thereby,
> Nor yet because who love Thee not
> Are lost eternally.'

## 2. Biblical teaching upholds the principle of justice

This is a second important principle behind the Bible's approach to reward and punishment. God is just, and a sense of justice seems to be part of that 'creation image' in which every man shares, so that 'getting your deserts' is a conviction natural to mankind. 'Punishment', wrote C. S. Lewis, 'is treating a person as a human being – giving him what he knows he deserves.' In a similar vein, the experts who combined to present the report on 'Punishment', published by the Church Information Office in 1963, concluded that criminals 'have a sense of justice that accepts a punishment which fits the crime, but rejects discrimination between those who commit the same offence'.

Throughout the New Testament, as well as the Old, comes the repeated assurance that because God is just, virtue will be rewarded and vice punished. There is a certain inevitability about it. 'God is not mocked, for whatever a man sows, that he will also reap' (Gal. 6: 7). Although, therefore, God's threats of punishment and promises of reward are bound to influence the behaviour of those who take them seriously, they cannot be put in the same category as the extra sweet a parent might offer – or

46

threaten to take away – to induce a small child to behave well when grandma comes. God's reward is not an added extra for good conduct, like some sort of bribe, nor is the punishment which Scripture describes in such terrifying terms merely the arbitrary threat of an offended deity. Both punishment and reward are set out as the inevitable consequences of what *will* happen in a morally-ordered universe, and the fact that the next life provides the setting for final judgment adds to the confidence man can have in the foolproof nature of God's justice. Even wrongs which escape the notice they deserve in this life will eventually be righted by the God who 'sees in secret' (Mt. 6: 4, 6, 17) and takes account of every careless word (Mt. 12: 36). He is absolutely just, and will not be deceived by human deviousness.

The *primary* purpose of Scripture, therefore, in setting out God's rewards and punishments so clearly is not to lure or terrify men into unwilling submission (though it may sometimes have that effect), but to dispel any uncertainty there might be in human minds about the eventual outcome of a life which is either God-centred or God-denying. Men *will* reap what they sow.

Some of the embarrassment modern readers feel with biblical teaching about heaven and hell is only a reflection of the movement away from the principle of retributive justice which is so marked in modern theories of penal reform. Sir John Anderson, for example, is quoted in the report of the Royal Commission on Capital Punishment (p. 196) as saying, 'There is no longer in our regard of the criminal law any recognition of such primitive conceptions as atonement or retribution.' The main trend today is to concentrate far more on remedial care for the offender, with far less insistence on a punishment that fits the crime. This accords very well with Jesus' sympathetic approach to sinners, but in His willingness to forgive He never called in question the clear retributive principle which undergirds

God's judgments. Retribution is the mainstay of justice, and those who would eliminate it altogether may find themselves trying to be more Christian than Christ. Christian teaching is that justice and mercy *meet* in Jesus, not that one must be *sacrificed* to make way for the other.

The Bible's teaching on reward and punishment must be viewed, therefore, against this backcloth of realism and justice. But there is also a third consideration which adds an exciting new dimension to the motivating forces the Bible brings into play.

### 3. Biblical teaching appeals to gratitude

If strict justice were God's sole concern in His dealings with men, the word 'reward' might drop out of the Bible's vocabulary altogether. Judged by merit alone, every man stands condemned by his sin. This was Jesus' conclusion. A condemned man cannot be released until the last penny of his debt has been paid, and no man has any hope of settling his debt with God (*cf.* Mt. 18: 33–35). Reprieve from punishment is through God's mercy alone. Similarly, no Christian servant can expect to *earn* any reward from God: 'When you have done all that is commanded you,' Jesus taught His disciples, 'say, "We are unworthy servants; we have only done what was our duty" ' (Lk. 17: 10).

Some of Jesus' parables illustrate the totally unmerited nature of the rewards God offers to His servants. The owner of the vineyard, for instance, paid the latecomers far more than they could reasonably have expected (Mt. 20: 1ff.), and the father laid on a feast for his prodigal son which he did not in the least deserve (Lk. 15: 22, 23). It is interesting to find in both stories that there were those who objected to such generosity on the grounds that it was unfair. God's 'rewards' far transcend the calls of strict justice.

This, of course, is nothing but the grace principle at work, God's undeserved love meeting man in his helpless need. Grace typified God's attitude to man from the day of creation. It was particularly vividly demonstrated in His choice of Israel as His covenant partner in Old Testament times, as Deuteronomy 7: 7, 8 makes clear: 'It was not because you were more in number than any other people that the LORD set his love upon you and chose you, for you were the fewest of all peoples; but it is because the LORD loves you.' Thus the laws of the covenant were firmly set in a covenant of grace. Regularly, when God laid a specific obligation on His people, it was prefaced by a mention of some undeserved act of loving-kindness they had received from Him and an invitation to them to respond gratefully. The Ten Commandments, for example, are introduced by a reminder of His special act of grace in rescuing Israel from slavery in Egypt (Ex. 20: 2). The detailed law-code of the book of Deuteronomy is preceded by four majestic chapters which unfold before the people all the many mighty works God has already done on their behalf; and it is in this setting that His demands are made.

The same pattern reappears in the New Testament too, especially in letters like Romans, Galatians and Ephesians where chapters which declare God's love and salvation in Jesus Christ are followed by urgent requests for faithful and grateful Christian conduct. And the way the ethical sections of these letters are made to depend on the theology which precedes them shows that Paul expected God's grace to supply the very *strongest* motive for Christian obedience. 'I appeal to you *therefore*, brethren, *by the mercies of God*, to present your bodies as a living sacrifice . . . ' (Rom. 12: 1).

The realism the Bible displays in appealing to man's profit-motive through its teaching on rewards and punishments is more than balanced by these invitations to live gratefully. For the Christian, God's love and grace provide the *main* impetus to right behaviour, over and above any fear of the consequences which disobedience may bring in its wake. This is a theme which threads its way through the whole of Scripture. Slaves must be treated generously, taught the Old Testament law, out of gratitude for the generous way God treated the people of Israel when they were slaves in Egypt (Dt. 15: 13–15). For similar reasons, businessmen must not weight their scales unfairly, and strangers must be looked after hospitably (Lv. 19: 34–36). Christians should love and give without looking for any returns, said Jesus, to show their gratitude for God's undeserved generosity to them. As they have freely received, so they must freely – and gratefully – give (Mt. 10: 8).

We are back, in fact, to the main theme of chapter 2. The God of the Bible is not a remote, impersonal deity who brings His mailed fist crashing down on the helpless heads of His victims with Dalek sadism, saying, 'I have authority. I have power. Obey me, or suffer.' He is the God of *personal relationship*, who says, 'Look at all I do for you. You are my people, I am your God. I love you, I care for you.' If we have known that love and care, we will want to reply, 'How can I possibly show my gratitude? I *long* to please you, God.'

Certainly there are promises of reward in Scripture, enticing carrots dangled in front of those who will submit and obey, just as there are penalties attached to disobedience which make it disadvantageous to rebel. Some people respond only to this kind of motivation (like those who will not stop their dogs fouling the footpath out of consideration for the neighbours, but are swayed by the threat of a fine). Men who are out of relationship with the Law-giver, and who find His rules coercive and burdensome, are the ones who will be influenced most by the prospect of rewards and punishments. But for those who live in close relationship with Him, there can be no greater reward than to please the one they love, and no greater pain than to cause Him displeasure.

The real stigma attached to disobedience in the Bible is not that it is disadvantageous, but that it is heart-breaking. In the story of the Fall, the result of man's sin was not a writ or a summons delivered by an angel from the heavenly attorney's office. God walked in the Garden, we are told, and called to Himself a couple who were too ashamed to face Him. Terrible penalties followed their act of disobedience, but the biggest tragedy of all was that a good relationship had been broken. Breaking God's law leads to broken hearts, and the desire to avert such a calamity is by far the most powerful obedience incentive to any man who already enjoys a close relationship with Him.

To sum up, then, the Bible gives two answers to the question, 'Why should I obey God's moral law?' At the very lowest level, all men should obey because it is to their ultimate advantage to do so. This is the way of 'carrot and stick'. But the second answer will carry far more weight for the Christian. The New Testament uses the same word for 'grace' and 'gratitude'. The clearer a Christian's insight into the undeserved love of God becomes, the stronger will be his desire to do God's will freely and gratefully from the heart.

# THE PLACE OF PLEASURE

As we have seen, biblical teaching about rewards and punishments makes a strong appeal to man's natural desire to gain pleasure for himself and to avoid pain. It is all part and parcel of the realistic approach to life that we find in the Bible. But the fact that this teaching looks mainly to the future (to concepts of heaven and hell which mark the ultimate in pleasure and pain) attracts a particular brand of criticism which has pursued the Christian church down through the ages. Christians, the critics claim, consistently display a *negative* attitude to the world in which they live. In their desire to have 'pie in the sky when they die', they heap together everything that other people regard as 'the good things of life' and label it all as vice which must be avoided in the interests of gaining the joys of eternal bliss. And the result is a rather grim, world-denying existence which makes a virtue of misery and does little to attract outsiders to the Christian faith. As one outsider, the poet Swinburne, witheringly accused Jesus, 'O pale Galilean, the world has grown grey from Thy breath.'

Joy Davidman tells a story in *Smoke on the Mountain* which illustrates this criticism admirably. A missionary was doing his best to convert an old African chief. 'I do not understand,' said the man at last. 'You tell me that I must not take my neighbour's wife.'

'That's right,' said the missionary.

'Or his ivory, or his oxen.'

'Quite right.'

'And I must not dance the war dance and then ambush him on the trail and kill him.'

'Absolutely right!'

'But I cannot do any of these things,' said the native regretfully. 'I am too old. To be old and to be a Christian, they are the same thing.'

'How many people', Miss Davidman concludes, 'picture Christianity as something old, sapless, joyless, mumbling in the chimney corner and casting sour looks at the young people's fun? How many think of religion as the enemy of life and the flesh and the pleasures of the flesh; a foe to all love and all delight? How many unconsciously conceive of God as rather like the famous old lady who said, "Find out what the baby's doing and make him stop"?'

The accusation is not that Christians are anti-pleasure of all sorts. If pleasure is defined as what a man does when he is doing what he likes, the Christian who enjoys worshipping God may find just as much pleasure in going to church, as the non-Christian who seeks his Sunday enjoyment in a trip to the coast. No man can blame his neighbour for failing to share his pleasures, because people differ enormously from one another in their opinions about what is pleasant and what is not. The kind of music (or sport or television programme) which brings great enjoyment to some, will be a cause of intense irritation to others. The point of the criticism is rather that Christians who cultivate their special other-worldly, 'spiritual' pleasures tend to disparage those who find enjoyment in such 'ordinary' things as material possessions, sex and alcohol. It is this negative, world-denying, ascetic attitude to the material pleasures of life which many non-Christians, and some Christians too, find so hard to appreciate.

## Pleasure in the Old Testament

Joy Davidman describes the missionary in her story as '*very Old Testament* – his version of Christianity leaned heavily on *thou-shalt-nots*'. Many would no doubt share the gloomy, kill-joy image she obviously has of Old Testament virtue, but a glance at the earlier pages of the Bible is enough to show that the attitude God's people adopted towards material pleasures was in fact very positive indeed. One quickly gathers that men such as Abraham, Moses and David would have been most astonished to learn that, in order to please God more, they ought to forgo the ordinary pleasures of life and take upon themselves monastic vows of poverty and celibacy.

If we take the case of *material possessions* as an example, it apparently seemed quite logical to Abraham's servant, sent to find Isaac a wife, to describe God's blessings to his master in material rather than spiritual terms. 'The LORD has greatly blessed my master,' he began, 'and he has become great; he has given him flocks and herds, silver and gold, menservants and maidservants, camels and asses' (Gn. 24: 35). Poverty was certainly no virtue to the patriarchs. A little later, the writer of Genesis explains how Isaac 'became rich, and gained more and more until he became very wealthy. He had possessions of flocks and herds, and a great household, so that the Philistines envied him.' And all these capital gains which made the neighbours so envious stemmed from the fact that 'the LORD blessed him' (Gn. 26: 12–14). Wealth was regarded in those days as evidence of God's special blessing, not as an impediment to a life devoted to His service.

The same positive note characterizes the Old Testament's approach to *sexual enjoyment*. The 'Acts of John', a later book with a pseudo-Christian label which was wisely relegated to the Apocrypha by the early canonists, describes sexual intercourse as 'an experiment of the serpent . . . the impediment which separates from the Lord'. As a commentary on the first chapters of Genesis, nothing could be less faithful to the biblical text. Genesis teaches that sex was one of God's gifts to man in his innocency, and therefore something thoroughly good (Gn. 1: 27, 31). Even after the Fall, when a sense of shame clouded sex for the first time, there is no disparagement of physical attractiveness. We can detect a note of admiration in the historian's descriptions both of Saul, the 'handsome young man', and of the rebel Absalom whose lengthy hairstyle (later to contribute to his downfall) meant that 'in all Israel there was no one so much to be praised for his beauty' (1 Sa. 9: 2; 2 Sa. 14: 25, 26). And the later writers of the Old Testament betray no shadow of embarrassment in teaching that the attractions of the opposite sex are to be welcomed and enjoyed. 'Rejoice in the wife of your youth,' advises the ever-practical book of Proverbs. 'Let her affection fill you at all times with delight, be infatuated always with her love' (Pr. 5: 18, 19). The Song of Solomon is perhaps best-known for its eulogies of physical love-making, and even solemn old Ecclesiastes unbends a little to advise the young married man 'Enjoy life with the wife whom you love, all the days of your vain life . . . ' (Ec. 9: 9).

The *celibate* finds little encouragement in the Old Testament, then, and there is plenty to distress the *teetotaller* too. Wine was part of Israel's staple diet, something which comes second only to love in its pleasure-giving potential according to the Song of Solomon (*cf.* Ct. 1: 2, 4; 7: 9). God causes 'the grass to grow for the cattle, and plants for man to cultivate', says the Psalmist, 'that he may bring forth food from the earth, and wine to gladden the heart of man' (Ps. 104: 14, 15; *cf.* Jdg. 9: 13). And once again Ecclesiastes has to agree: 'Go, eat your bread with enjoyment, and drink your wine with a merry heart. . . . Bread is made for laughter, and wine gladdens life' (Ec. 9: 7; 10: 19).

There is, of course, another side to the picture which the Old Testament does not neglect to paint in faithfully. *Excessive* drinking is a menace. 'Wine is a mocker, strong drink a brawler; and whoever is led astray by it is not wise' (Pr. 20: 1). The sex urge, too, can lead a man astray, as David found to his cost when lust for Bathsheba led him to send her husband to his death (2 Sa. 11). And coveting another man's possessions was a common enough failing to merit a special place among the prohibitions of the Ten Commandments. Any one of God's gifts can be abused. But the Bible does not draw the conclusion that because abuse is widespread, total abstinence is therefore the best policy. While all abuses are condemned in plain, strong language, the proper use of material things which God has provided for man's enjoyment is constantly encouraged. The Old Testament does not perhaps go quite so far as the rabbi who said that each individual will be called to account for every good thing he might have enjoyed and did not enjoy, but on page after page we meet a full-blooded, godly exultation in the pleasant things of life.

## Monks and hermits

If, then, there is very little in the Old Testament to encourage the man who would regard it as a Christian duty to turn his back on material things, how are we to account for the very strong ascetic tradition which has always influenced, and sometimes dominated, Christian moral teaching?

The answer is to be found in the history-books of the church, rather than in the Bible. The monks and hermits of the fourth and fifth centuries, for example, set a pattern of extreme abstinence which excited the admiration of their Christian contemporaries, but would almost certainly have led to their excommunication as Marcionites three hundred years before. (Marcion had tried to make abstinence from marriage, wine and private possessions a condition of church membership, and was branded as a heretic.) They did all they could think of to cut themselves loose from worldly desires. Some would not bath, to avoid seeing their naked bodies; as Jerome wrote to a convert in Rome, 'Why should Paula add fuel to a sleeping fire by taking a bath?' Private possessions were gladly surrendered, and family ties ruthlessly severed. William Barclay tells the story of a Christian called Mucius who entered a monastery with his eight-year-old son. To test his father's vocation, the boy was taken away and systematically beaten. The monks were delighted with their new postulant: 'The love of Christ conquered, nor did he grieve over the lad's injuries.' As a final test, Mucius was ordered to throw his son into the river. And this 'new Abraham' would actually have done so, we are proudly told, if the monks had not stopped him.

Despite the allusion to Genesis, all this is very foreign to the spirit of biblical teaching. It was at this early stage of Christian history, too, that the idea of the *double standard* gained wide currency. Having possessions, getting married and raising a family were accepted as things an ordinary Christian might be allowed to do, but it was assumed that any man or woman who wanted to live at the very highest for the Lord would naturally prefer to renounce all sources of material pleasure and enter a monastery or convent. In university terms, taking monastic vows was reckoned to make all the difference between a 'pass' and 'honours' in the Christian moral life.

## Pleasure in the New Testament

Such negative attitudes are certainly a far cry from the strongly 'world-affirming' approach of the Old Testament, but there have been many Christians in the history of the church who have chosen to lead an ascetic life in the firm belief that, by so doing, they are faithfully following the example of *Jesus Himself*. It was Jesus' command to the rich young ruler, 'Sell all that you have,' that launched Francis of Assisi on his ministry. In his biography of Francis, G. K. Chesterton contrasts the unhappiness of the man in the Gospels who found this command too much for him, with the great joy Francis experienced as he took the Lord at His word: 'He went out half-naked into the winter woods, walking the frozen ground between frosty trees; a man without a father. He was penniless, he was parentless, he was to all appearance without a trade or a plan or a hope in the world; and as he went under the frosty trees, *he burst suddenly into song.*'

Francis, no doubt, saw much in his own self-imposed poverty which matched the example of his Lord, who 'thought he was rich, yet for your sake became poor' (2 Cor. 8: 9). In leaving home to exercise a wandering ministry he could also point to the Son of man who had 'nowhere to lay his head' (Lk. 9: 58). And was it not Jesus Himself who said, when members of His family were asking for Him, 'whoever does the will of God is my brother, and sister, and mother' (Mk. 3: 31–35)? There even seems to be a hint of monastic 'double standard' teaching in the rich young ruler episode, as Matthew describes it. Jesus' instruction to the young man, 'Go, sell what you possess,' is prefaced by the words, 'If you would be *perfect*' (Mt. 19: 21). Did not Jesus imply a difference here between 'perfect' Christians who renounce everything, and merely 'adequate' disciples who feel they cannot go quite so far? Some would certainly see a 'double standard' allusion, as well as an encouragement for the Christian celibate, in the rather strange sayings which Matthew records immediately after Jesus' teaching on divorce and remarriage. 'There are eunuchs', said Jesus, 'who have been so from birth, and there are eunuchs who have been made eunuchs by men, and there are eunuchs who have made themselves eunuchs for the sake of the kingdom of heaven' (Mt. 19: 12). If the first phrase refers to sexual incapacity, and the second to sterilization, can the third be a reference to Christian celibacy? And when Jesus concluded, 'He who is *able to receive this*, let him receive it,' did He not mean that celibacy was an ideal to which only 'top-class' Christians could hope to aspire?

While some have found asceticism in Jesus' teaching and example, many more have confidently labelled Paul as the arch-ascetic of the Christian faith. An apostle who could tell 'those who have wives' to 'live as though they had none', and 'those who buy' to behave 'as though they had no goods' (1 Cor. 7: 29, 30) certainly sounds very much like the forerunner of men like Mucius who deliberately cut themselves off from family ties and financial concerns in the name of Christ. Hugh Hefner, founder of *Playboy* magazine and chief prophet of the aggressively hedonistic philosophy expounded in its editorial columns, brands Paul as the man chiefly responsible for the puritanical, anti-sexual views which (in Hefner's opinion) riddle the modern church. He strings together some verses from the Epistles to prove that Paul had a sexual hang-up: 'It is well for a man not to touch a woman. . . . For I know that nothing good dwells within me, that is, in my flesh. . . . Wretched man that I am! Who will deliver me from this body of death?' Jesus, Hefner is convinced, would much prefer a job with *Playboy* magazine, if He were alive on earth today, than a position on the ministerial staff of a 'joy-killing, pleasure-denying, fundamentalist church' which leaned too heavily on Paul's ascetic diatribes.

This, however, is a vicious parody of Paul's teaching. Hefner has joined together verses from two different Epistles (Romans and 1 Corinthians) with a cheerful disregard for subject and context which would do credit to an unscrupulous news editor bent on character assassination. In the passage from Romans, Paul is not writing specifically about sex at all. In 1 Corinthians 7, the second passage, his main aim is to counter *anti*-sex teaching at Corinth. The words Hefner quotes are in all probability an expression of the opinion Paul was combating. He acknowledges that in days of persecution, marriage involves extra worries which the unmarried do well to escape, and he recognizes that God calls some not to get married at all. But for those deeply in love who are 'aflame with passion', it is *better* to marry, in his opinion (v. 9). Marriage is not sin (v. 28); and those who are married must not deny to their partners full conjugal rights (vv. 3–5). Paul was no ascetic in his views on sex, or on anything else for that matter. In a later letter he publicly disassociated himself from 'liars whose consciences are seared, who forbid marriage and enjoin abstinence from foods which God created to be received with thanksgiving by those who believe and know the truth'. 'For everything created by God is good,' he concluded, 'and nothing is to be rejected if it is received with thanksgiving' (1 Tim. 4: 2–4).

There is an interesting link between Paul's advice to the unmarried at Corinth and Jesus' teaching about celibacy (if that is the right interpretation of the 'eunuch' passage). Both are set in a marriage context, and in both cases there is a reference to God's 'gift' (1 Cor. 7: 7; Mt. 19: 11). The meaning seems clear. Those who have been granted the gift of celibacy should not hanker after marriage; they are in a position to serve their Lord in ways not open to the married. And the reverse is equally true. A couple who are 'gifted' with marriage should not be ashamed of their feelings for each other, or hanker after the gift of celibacy (as some at Corinth apparently were). It is a mark of immaturity to disdain one's own gifts and envy others, or to suppose that one is superior to another.

Jesus, then, was no more of an ascetic than Paul. The rich young man was told to renounce his possessions because, *in his case*, the things he possessed stood between him and full

Christian commitment, not because being wealthy was something wrong in itself. Similarly, Jesus put His relatives second only when family interests threatened to interfere with His primary responsibility to do the Father's will – not because He considered it in some way 'super-spiritual' to renounce family life. Indeed on other occasions we find Him criticizing those who tried to evade their family responsibilities on religious grounds (Mk. 7: 11); and on the cross we see Him making time to provide for His mother's future security (Jn. 19: 26). Although His public ministry demanded constant travel without a settled home, Jesus never led a truly ascetic life. He showed His concern for people's *physical* needs by healing their bodies, as well as preaching to their souls. He was glad to join in the wedding festivities at Cana, and (even worse from an ascetic's viewpoint) provided more wine when supplies ran out at the reception (Jn. 2: 1–10). He entered into social life so freely that He was criticized for being 'a glutton and a drunkard' (Mt. 11: 19) by those with greater inhibitions than He.

## Understanding pleasure

New Testament teaching does not cramp the Christian's enjoyment of life. In fact, it actually broadens our understanding of pleasure in two important ways. In the first place, it insists that *the interests of other people* must be brought into full consideration, if our personal pleasure is to be fully genuine. Jesus taught that a life of practical love for others – which meant putting their interests first – would lead to 'full' joy for those who gave, as well as for those who received (Jn. 15: 10–12). In his farewell speech at Ephesus, Paul quoted some more words of Jesus which make the same point: 'I have shown you', he said, 'that by so toiling one must help the weak, remembering the words of the Lord Jesus, how he said, "It is more blessed to give than to receive"' (Acts 20: 35). The word for 'blessed' in that saying means 'happy'. The route to true happiness, according to Christian teaching, lies through giving loving service to others.

The same truth can, of course, be put in a negative form, and the New Testament does not hesitate to do this when the occasion demands it. So Paul condemns indulgence in any pleasure which is likely to be a source of moral or spiritual danger to others. Some 'innocent' pleasures play on other people's weaknesses. In such cases love dictates self-restraint. It would not be very loving, for example, for a man who saw nothing wrong in the occasional drink to indulge his pleasure in the presence of an alcoholic. 'Take care', writes Paul, 'lest this liberty of yours somehow become a stumbling block to the weak' (1 Cor. 8: 9). 'It is right not to eat meat or drink wine *or do anything* that makes your brother stumble' (Rom. 14: 21). If selfish enjoyment is spurious pleasure, the Christian will gladly surrender the counterfeit for the genuine article, which comes only through selfless love.

Many non-Christian hedonists have seen and accepted this truth. Jeremy Bentham and John Stuart Mill are just two well-known figures from the past who became outstanding philanthropists, while professing to follow a hedonistic philosophy which put personal pleasure first. The main difference between their approach and the New Testament's lies in motivation. The thinking hedonist serves others only because he realizes that his own happiness largely depends on his relationships with them. If he behaves in a selfish, unscrupulous way, those around him will be alienated, and eventually he will suffer himself. So he becomes a philanthropist. The Christian, on the other hand, is called upon to love other people without expecting any returns for himself (Lk. 6: 32–35; 14: 12–14).

Among contemporary hedonists, Hugh Hefner of *Playboy* has made a greater impact on the popular mind than most, in publicizing his views on 'recreational sex'. Although Hefner strongly denies the charges of irresponsible hedonism that are frequently made against him, he freely admits that self-fulfilment is the chief goal of *Playboy* ethics, and he storms against those who preach self-denial in place of self-gratification. If the Playboy shows consideration for his 'Playmate', it is only to advance his own ends. Other people are valued only in so far as they serve his own pleasure. When they no longer do so, they may be gently – but firmly – jettisoned. This is really nothing more than the law of the jungle in sophisticated dress. As one of Hefner's American critics has pointed out, there are few things more self-fulfilled than a tiger or a python that has just feasted on its prey; and it does not make much difference if the tiger is wearing the latest cashmere sweater!

The Bible's definition of pleasure is too big to allow for anything less than *joy through love*. New Testament writers forbid fornication not because they are against the joys and pleasures of life, but because treating other people as playthings and not as persons is too narrow a description of 'enjoyment' to be tolerated on Christian grounds. 'For *Playboy*'s man', writes Harvey Cox, 'others – especially women – are for him. They are his leisure accessories, his playthings. For the Bible, man only becomes fully man by being *for* the other . . . if Christians bear the name of One who was truly man because He was totally for the other, and if it is in Him that we know who God is and what human life is for, then we must see in *Playboy* the latest and slickest episode in man's continuing refusal to be fully human.'[1]

The second main way in which Scripture broadens the dictionary definition of pleasure is by insisting that *all genuine enjoyment derives from God*. Any pleasure from which God is excluded is a debasing of the term, according to the Bible. This sometimes seems to have the effect of con-

[1] Harvey Cox, *The Secular City* (SCM, 1965), p. 204.

trasting the ordinary pleasures of life with the special joys God promises to those who obey Him. Real joy, as Scripture defines it, consists of so much more than the temporary, spasmodic kicks which are all that material sources of pleasure have to offer, once God is left out of the reckoning. Jesus warned that 'a man's life does not consist in the abundance of his possessions', and after telling the parable of the rich fool whose life philosophy was 'take your ease, eat, drink, be merry', He encouraged His hearers to be 'rich *toward God*' and not lay up treasures for themselves (Lk. 12: 15–21). The Epistle to the Hebrews points out that Jesus practised what He preached in this respect. Because of His life's work he chose to forgo many ordinary pleasures and to suffer a good deal of pain; and it was 'for the joy that was set before him' that 'he endured the cross, despising the shame' (Heb. 12: 2). If a choice has to be made between so-called enjoyment of life *without* God now, and the joys of eternity in obedience to His will, Jesus was in no doubt as to which a man in his right mind would choose (*cf.* Mt. 18: 8, 9).

The contrast between material and spiritual pleasures is, however, more apparent than real. As both Creator and Redeemer, God means man to enjoy the material pleasures of creation as well as the spiritual pleasures of redemption. The only proviso is that he acknowledges the source of his enjoyment, that it is 'God who richly furnishes us with everything to enjoy' (1 Tim. 6: 17). The Old Testament patriarchs saw this with particular clarity. They prized material goods, but they never lost sight of the fact that the things they enjoyed were practical evidence of God's favour. These men were certainly not ascetics, but they were not materialists either – unlike some of their successors who (like Achan and Saul) set material gain above God's will, and discovered that such disobedience eventually brought them more pain than pleasure. Concentrating on the pleasure, while disregarding its true source, is about as silly, according to Scripture, as cutting down the tree in order to get at the fruit. In fact 'enjoying yourself' outside God's will is an expression that cries out to be put in inverted commas, because it does not measure up to the high biblical standard of enjoyment at all. True pleasure, like everything else that is good, must be God-centred. As the Psalmist sang, '*In thy presence* there is fullness of joy, *in thy right hand* are pleasures for evermore' (Ps. 16: 11).

In discovering the right place for pleasure, then, the Christian has two sets of critics to answer. *The ascetic* advises a much stronger stand against worldly pleasures. His case receives a boost today from the revolt against western materialism, with its glorification of the transient and the trivial, which has found expression in the resurgence of interest in eastern religions like Buddhism. 'We seek not that which we despise, that is worldly prosperity and success,' writes Christmas Humphreys, QC, a leading English Buddhist. To him the Christian would reply that salvation does not come through extinction of desire. The pleasures of the world are not to be renounced as an essential preliminary for gaining a clear vision of God. It was God Himself who created them, and He means them to be enjoyed in a spirit of thankfulness.

At the other extreme stands *the hedonist* who reproaches the Christian for his prudery and scoffs at his self-restraint. 'Break free from your inhibitions', laughs *Playboy*, 'and learn to enjoy life.' To Hugh Hefner and his friends the biblical answer is that genuine freedom to enjoy life comes only through loving God, who is the source of all true pleasure, and serving others. In the words of the New Testament, 'Live as free men, yet without using your freedom as a pretext for evil; but *live as servants of God*.' 'For you were called to freedom, brethren; only do not use your freedom as an opportunity for the flesh, but *through love be servants of one another*' (1 Pet. 2: 16; Gal. 5: 13). It is one of the strange facts of life that those who spend all their time and energy in pursuing pleasure rarely find the lasting happiness they crave. Genuine joy is a by-product, the overflow of a life spent in putting God and other people firmly before self.

# PRIVATE AND PUBLIC

## The failure to get involved

On Good Friday, 1964, in a respectable area of New York City, Catherine Genovese, a decent, pretty young woman of twenty-eight, was stalked through the streets on her way home to her apartment and was stabbed again and again by a man who had followed her and who took almost half an hour to kill her. Catherine screamed repeatedly for help. 'Oh, my God! He stabbed me! Please help me! Someone help me!' she was heard to cry out.

At least thirty-eight people, peering through their apartment windows, witnessed this gruesome murder, but not one lifted a finger to help; not one bothered even to telephone the police. One spectator finally telephoned his friend in another State to tell what he was seeing and to ask, 'What shall I do?' When told to notify the police, he walked to another building, knocked at the door of an elderly lady's apartment and asked *her* to telephone the police. This she did, and within minutes the police arrived. But Catherine Genovese was already dead.

When the thirty-eight witnesses, all 'respectable' citizens, were asked later *why* they had done nothing, the answer came from one person after another, 'I just didn't want to get involved.' Here was a woman in desperate peril. At least thirty-eight persons saw and recognized her need, but they 'just didn't want to get involved'.[1]

This horrifying incident reads like a modern version of the parable of the Good Samaritan, but with an unhappy (and more realistic?) ending. It illustrates the lonely individualism which permeates western society today, when elderly people can lie dead for weeks in their basement rooms without anyone noticing, and families in high-rise London blocks do not even know the surname of their next-door neighbours. Perhaps the most terrifying thing about Catherine Genovese's fate was the way 'respectable' people pleaded 'not wanting to get involved' as their excuse for witnessing a human tragedy and doing nothing about it. We are not told how many of the thirty-eight witnesses were churchgoers (though by the law of averages it is likely that several were), but we are only too familiar with the definition of respectability, to be found inside the church as well as outside it, which excludes any personal involvement in social need – apart, perhaps, from taking a vague interest in the international news and dropping a few coins in a collection box at Christmas time.

Jesus, too, was familiar with this isolationist view of respectability, and He made no secret of His opposition to it. He mixed openly with social outcasts Himself, despite the raised eyebrows of those who apparently valued their reputations more highly than He did. 'Go and do likewise,' He commanded the man whose question sparked off the story about the Good Samaritan. Very pointedly, He told about the rich man who did no harm to the sore-infested beggar at his gate, but gave him no material assistance either, and was condemned by God for his *failure to help*. At the last judgment, Jesus taught, there will be those who address God as 'Lord', but who have already demonstrated the spuriousness of their faith by failing to get involved with

[1] I owe the account of this incident to Dr Kenneth Scott's booklet, *The New Era in Medical Missions* (IVP, 1965).

the needs of the socially deprived. 'I was hungry and you gave me no food, I was thirsty and you gave me no drink, I was a stranger and you did not welcome me, naked and you did not clothe me, sick and in prison and you did not visit me' (Mt. 25: 42, 43).

## Love your neighbour

Jesus' plain speaking about the need for social involvement is all the more remarkable because He was not talking to people who had any reason to confuse respectability with isolationism. The Jews to whom He spoke were men and women of the Old Testament, and the Old Testament clearly taught that participation in God's covenant was not merely a religious matter. As well as joining the individual to his God in a new relationship, the old covenant also bound its fellow-members to one another with the closest of ties. The vertical bond between God and man was complemented by a horizontal bond between man and man, and the prophets in particular are scathing in their condemnation of those who pretended to be religious while turning a blind eye to social injustice. 'I hate, I despise your feasts, and I take no delight in your solemn assemblies,' thunders Amos (speaking in God's name). 'Take away from me the noise of your songs; to the melody of your harps I will not listen. But let justice roll down like waters, and righteousness like an ever-flowing stream' (Am. 5: 21, 23, 24). 'He has showed you, O man, what is good,' declared Micah; 'and what does the LORD require of you but to do justice, and to love kindness, and to walk humbly with your God?' (Mi. 6: 8). Any idea of moral goodness which excludes concern for social justice is not only false; it is *ungodly*, according to the Old Testament prophets.

It was this strong sense of community that led to the deep social concern which characterizes the Old Testament law.

In the one close community unit, each individual member had his rights, and the weak and the underprivileged came under the special protection of covenant legislation. Detailed regulations safeguarded the interests of the widow and the orphan, the stranger and the poor (Ex. 22 and 23). Those with physical disabilities were not to be victimized either; the deaf man must not be cursed, nor the blind tripped up (Lv. 19: 14). Even the slave was not forgotten. The Ten Commandments recognized his need for rest, and in the year of release (when every Hebrew slave must be offered his freedom), no man was to be dismissed empty-handed; 'you shall furnish him liberally out of your flock, out of your threshing floor, and out of your wine press; as the LORD your God has blessed you, you shall give to him' (Dt. 15: 13, 14).

In some minds, the Old Testament social legislation may have encouraged *too narrow* an idea of community. It was true that all God's covenant people lived under the same law, and partiality to anyone on account of wealth or social standing was ruled out absolutely. The same privileges were extended to the 'sojourner' too. But it was permissible to treat the out-and-out *foreigner* a little less generously. Interest might be charged on a loan to a 'foreigner' but not on one to a 'brother', said the law (Dt. 23: 20). So too, a foreigner's debts must still be paid when the year of release arrived, unlike those of a 'neighbour' which must be remitted (Dt. 15: 1–3). Before such acts of discrimination are condemned too heavily, however, they must be seen in their correct perspective. No foreigner was denied his full human rights under Israelite law. What he did *not* receive was what Derek Kidner calls the 'brotherly bonus' to which the sojourner and the full covenant member were entitled under the provisions of the 'year of release'.[2] The difference is really analogous to that between ordinary, fair commercial trading practice, and the special terms a businessman

[2] F. D. Kidner, *Hard Sayings* (IVP, 1972), p. 29.

might offer (an interest-free loan, perhaps) to those especially close to him.

Whatever the reasons behind the Old Testament's treatment of the foreigner, the smouldering fires of racial prejudice are quickly fanned into flame, and by Jesus' time there were those who interpreted Old Testament 'neighbour-love' in a very narrow way. No effort would be spared to help a fellow-Jew in trouble, but with a Gentile it was a different matter. William Barclay quotes one rabbinic saying to the effect that 'the daughter of an Israelite may not assist a Gentile woman in childbirth since she would be assisting to bring to birth a child for idolatry'. There seems to have been very little in the way of *colour* prejudice in New Testament times, but *racial* discrimination by Jews against Gentiles was rife.

Both in His teaching (as in the parable of the Good Samaritan) and in His actions (in asking the Samaritan woman at the well of Sychar for a drink, for example), Jesus made it quite plain that neighbour-love, as He understood it, recognized no barriers of race or sex. God's love is for the *world* (Jn. 3: 16), and the Christian's concern for society must be no less wide.

It is interesting to notice that the word used for 'love' in the Gospels (*agapē*) is hardly found at all in Greek literature outside the New Testament. It is almost as though Jesus wanted to distinguish linguistically between the all-embracing neighbour-love He was commending, and any other narrower attitude or sentiment loosely called 'love' in ordinary conversation. In every way, *agapē*'s horizons are broader than those of any other kind of love. Physical passion, for example, is not decried in the Bible, but *erōs* is basically a response to someone else who is found attractive; while *agapē* goes much further, *loving* those whom it is impossible to *like*, even one's enemies (Lk. 6: 35). Again, friendship (*philia*) must be reciprocated if it is to survive; but *agapē* goes on loving even when its advances are refused

71

(*cf*. Rom. 5: 8). Family affection (*storgē*) is another kind of love, but its benefits are restricted to the members of a particular group; *agapē*, on the other hand, responds to need wherever it finds it, whether inside the family circle or not.

It is to such far-reaching *agapē*-love, reflecting as it does the all-embracing love of God displayed by Christ, that the Christian is called in his relationships with other people. During a recent visit of Russian leaders to Canada, one banner carried by a demonstrator read 'Jesus loves you, Mr Kosygin'. Reporting this, one newspaperman added that the Russians were 'apparently not worried'. One senses the tongue-in-cheek humour of the reporter, but there is surely a touch of sadness in the whole little episode, when men so devoted to the ideals of social betterment should turn their backs on such a power-source of community compassion as the *agapē* of Christ.

## A kid-gloved approach?

Perhaps the Bible draws closer to the spirit of the twentieth century in its insistence on social justice than in almost any other way. People today are passionately concerned about social justice (though some of the more vocal protesters show more concern for distant issues than they do for the less spectacular responsibilities on their doorsteps, which is a feeble caricature of biblical *neighbour*-love). It is one of the strange features of our times that while permissiveness in inter-personal relationships is widespread, there is an out-spoken intolerance, especially among students, for any persecution of minority interests. A cinema may feature homosexuality on the screen and attract very little criticism; but if a neighbouring theatre puts on a play which extols the principle of apartheid the manager can expect violent demonstrations before the end of his first week. Political sensitivities run high. Few modern ministers would invite their congregations to sing the hymn 'All things bright and beautiful', without first cutting out the verse which begins –

'The rich man in his castle,
The poor man at his gate,
God made them high and lowly
And ordered their estate.'

Words written in all innocence and sincerity as an expression of worship not so very many years ago now strike a painful spot on our social consciences.

So far has the pendulum swung from 'private' to 'public' morality, that while the controls Scripture imposes on personal behaviour are considered far too stifling, the Bible disappoints many radicals by its apparently kid-gloved approach to the corrupt institutions of society. Jesus, say His modern critics, did not go nearly far enough in His fight for social justice. He had a great many compassionate things to say to the deprived and down-trodden. He also had some sharp words for the representatives of the selfish rich, and for members of the hypocritical religious establishment. But He *did* virtually nothing to change the social institutions which lay behind all the unfairness and the suffering He was trying to alleviate. He might well have taken a leaf out of the book of the Omega organization which insisted on carrying relief supplies into Bangladesh, in defiance of a government order, at the time of the India-Pakistan war. 'We're not a relief organisation,' said an Omega spokesman in a radio interview. 'We're more an act of interference.' Jesus may have brought *relief* to many sufferers, it is suggested, but He did very little to *interfere* with the established sources of social injustice from which this suffering and exploitation arose. And His followers' record is really no better. Paul, instead of challenging the institution of slavery as he ought, contented himself with advising masters and slaves on the way they should behave towards one another. Peter, when he had every reason to start an underground movement to counter political oppression, urged his people instead to 'be subject for the Lord's sake to every human institution' (1 Pet. 2: 13). It is no wonder, with such examples to follow, that the church has consistently shown itself to be a supporter of the socio-political *status quo*.

Such criticisms are helpful because they throw into sharper focus the distinctive approach the New Testament adopts towards social issues. It is not altogether fair to say that Jesus and His first disciples made no impact at all on the society of their day (Jesus' action in turning profiteers out of the Temple can hardly be labelled meek social acquiescence, and, as Acts 17: 6 reminds us, the early disciples quickly gained for themselves the reputation of those who had 'turned the world upside down'); but it is still true that on some occasions the early Christians, following Jesus' example, deliberately held back from open confrontations with established authority. Civil disturbances often followed the apostles' preaching, but we never hear that it was incited by the Christians themselves. In the very early days after Pentecost the disciples defied the authority of the Sanhedrin, but they did not follow up their action by rallying support for a violent demonstration at the Temple gates. They suffered the painful consequences of their act of civil disobedience quietly, and then rejoiced 'that they were counted worthy to suffer dishonour for the name' (Acts 5: 41). Even in the book of Revelation, with its strongly-worded denunciations of the persecuting state power, we find the saints preparing for martyrdom, not for revolution. Is such a low-key reaction a proper sign of Christian meekness – or a mark of blameworthy human weakness in the face of conventions and institutions which should have been challenged, not condoned?

Three important considerations underlie the answer.

## 1. Biblical realism

In the first place, as we have already seen, *the Bible is realistic in its approach to problems of behaviour*. Jesus Himself, with legions of angels at His command (Mt. 26: 53), could have withstood the political forces of Rome single-handed (though in the interests of His life's purpose He chose not to make use of the power He had). But for the first Christians it was very different. With few exceptions, they were men and women drawn from the lower ranks of society. Living under a totalitarian regime, they had no political influence to wield, as they might have had under a democracy, and anything they were able to do to rectify social evils on a world scale was negligible. But what they *could* do was to demonstrate the power of Christian love within the context of those non-ideal social circumstances they were powerless to change, and it is here that the main emphasis of the New Testament falls. Paul's conviction was that the institution of slavery, for example, with all its inbuilt inequalities and injustices, could be transformed if both masters and servants were gripped by the love of Christ. In the same way, Christians might not be able to do anything to bring down the government, but in their attitudes to state officials they could do a very great deal to advertise their Master's standards. And this kind of approach was far from being a weak capitulation to the *status quo*. The seeds for social change in Paul's words to the Christians in Galatia, for instance ('There is neither Jew nor Greek, there is neither slave nor free, there is neither male nor female; for you are all one in Christ Jesus' – Gal. 3: 28), are still bearing fruit 1900 years later. But the New Testament teaches Christians to balance idealistic goals with practical realism in daily living. In C. E. B. Cranfield's wise words, 'the Christian should be aware of the danger of being so preoccupied with the quest of the unattainable that he fails to achieve the limited goals that are within his reach.'

## 2. Changing human nature

Secondly, *Jesus was more radical in His attitude to social change* than some of His modern critics. T. W. Manson points out that whenever there is a project for some kind of community improvement (the provision of better housing, for example), almost certainly two voices will be heard in the discussion. 'One says that the only way to make the slum-dweller better is to remove him from his present environment and put him into better surroundings. It is urged that if you do that and give him a fair chance in a better house with proper amenities and pleasant surroundings, he will adapt himself to his new environment and become a respectable citizen. The other voice, less hopeful, says that if you put the slum-dweller into a better environment, before very long he will be storing an extra coal supply in the bath and cutting up the banisters for firewood; and in a few months he will have brought his new house down to the level of the property which he has just left. One party or group says: "If you want people to live better, you must improve their living conditions"; the other says: "If you want to improve conditions, you must have better people." '[3]

It would be wrong to polarize these alternatives too sharply, but Jesus seems to have adopted the second approach rather than the first. His method was not to tackle social evils in their institutional shape and form. He preferred to work through individuals into society, rather than vice versa, in the belief that to get a changed environment you need changed people. So we find Him dealing directly with Zacchaeus, the tax-collector of Jericho, insteading of issuing a general manifesto denouncing financial corruption in high places. Above all, Jesus sought to bring individual men and women into full commitment to God, knowing that genuine faith would lead to far-reaching social con-

[3] T. W. Manson, *Ethics and the Gospel* (SCM, 1960), p. 12.

sequences. And history amply illustrates how religious conversion does in fact bring a new social alertness. Periods of revival in religious faith have usually been followed by periods of beneficial social change. Evangelistic agencies like the Billy Graham Evangelistic Association report that old debts have been paid, race relations improved, and stolen property returned, in cities where crusades have recently been held. And in the more remote corners of the world, Christian missionary societies have a far finer record for improving living conditions among those whom they evangelize, than any other philanthropic organizations.

Does this mean that Jesus would have taken no part in the protest movements of today? Would He have sought interviews with prominent racialists rather than joined in anti-apartheid marches? It is tempting to draw this kind of conclusion, but it would be dangerous to do so. Modern conditions and opportunities are very different from those of Gospel times, and speculation about what Jesus *would* have done is idle. All we can do is to take notice of the way He *did* approach social evils in the circumstances of His own day, and underline the truth that the only radical solutions to social problems are those that bring a change in human nature. Writing as Director General of the British National Economic Development Council, Sir Frederick Catherwood says, 'The problems of this age are not technical. . . . If you look at the economy of any country and you begin to probe the reasons for slow progress; if you try to find why personal income instead of rising at 10 per cent per annum rises only at 4 or 2 per cent or not at all, then you very quickly discover that the reasons are not technical but human.'[4] Much the same can be said about any social issue. In the New Testament, James asks a rhetorical question which lies behind the protests of all anti-war movements. 'What causes wars, and what causes fightings

[4] H. F. R. Catherwood, *The Christian Citizen* (Hodder and Stoughton, 1970), p. 36.

among you? Is it not your passions that are at war in your members? You desire and do not have; so you kill. And you covet and cannot obtain; so you fight and wage war' (Jas. 4: 1, 2). We need a new society, but we cannot have a new society without new people.

## 3. Shaking the foundations

The third attitude which characterizes the Bible's approach to social change is *caution*. Marghanita Laski, the humanist, once confessed in an interview that she found it easy to protest against what she disliked in society, but far harder to set out her own blueprint for an ideal world. This is the predicament many social rebels face. It is far easier to scrawl 'Burn it all down' on a wall (and, indeed, to carry the threat into action) than to work constructively and positively towards social improvement. Jesus was not blind to the powerful pressures which can so easily frustrate a keen social conscience (He knew all about political leaders who 'lord it' over those they should be serving; *cf.* Mk. 10: 42), but He nevertheless showed a great deal of respect for the main structures of society.

The Bible teaches that certain social patterns are basic to God's creation-plan. Sometimes they are described in terms of *relationships*. There is the relationship man has with all the rest of creation, for example, and the man-to-man relationships of government and work, of marriage and family life. And it is also possible to view these basic social patterns as *authority structures*, because built into each relationship, according to the Bible, is a pattern of leadership. So man is entrusted with 'dominion' over the rest of creation (Gn. 1: 28); the husband is the 'head' of the wife (Eph. 5: 23); children must 'obey' their parents, and slaves must 'be obedient' to their masters (Eph. 6: 1, 5);[5]

---

[5] The institution of slavery, very different from that of eighteenth-century Britain, provided the most obvious labour relationship of New Testament times.

and 'every person' must be 'subject to the governing authorities' (Rom. 13: 1).

There is no reason why the presence of this fundamental authority structure should in any way mar the quality of the relationships involved, any more than the presence of law must inevitably spoil the expression of love; but in practical living this is unfortunately what happens all too frequently. Authority is abused, and relationships are spoiled. Man exploits his dominion over nature selfishly, and provokes ecological crises. Husbands fail to love their wives 'as Christ loved the church and gave himself up for her' (Eph. 5: 25), and, as a result, marriages are spoiled. Fathers give such a false idea of parenthood to their children that Sunday School teachers have to exercise the greatest care in teaching them the beginning of the Lord's Prayer. Employers act like gods (if they are allowed to), forgetting that they 'also have a Master in heaven' (Col. 4: 1); and government officials dominate those whom they are meant to lead in service. And the natural end result of such feudalism, paternalism and authoritarianism is a general disillusionment with all the inbuilt authority structures of society, and a longing to be set free from their bondage, so that a fresh start can be made.

However natural such extreme reactions may be, they are not in man's best interests, according to the Bible. These 'creation relationships', complete with their authority structures, are so fundamental to life as God has planned it that they cannot simply be scrapped and replaced by something better. There *is* nothing better. Hence the extreme caution the New Testament displays on the subject of rebellion against established authority. 'God is not a God of confusion, but of peace,' Paul reminds the Christians at Corinth, where authority in the church was on the verge of breaking down. Anarchy in any department of life is anathema to Him. Christians are called upon to *improve* the basic relationships on which society rests, but not to *destroy* them.

They are to be not only 'the light of the world', witnessing to the highest social ideals, but also 'the salt of the earth', preserving all that is worth while in God's creation pattern. Any threat to that pattern must be stoutly resisted, whether to the balance of creation through the rise of neo-pantheism, to family stability through demands for easy divorce and abortion, or to state authority by blind revolution. Abuse of authority must be exposed and (wherever possible) eradicated, but to attempt to eliminate authority-structures from life completely is to cut the seams God has stitched together to hold the fabric of society in place.


## A God-centred approach

This blend, then, between radical outrage at unfair practices and conservative respect for the institutions which hold society together, characterizes the Bible's approach to social issues. But overshadowing them all is the conviction which forms the main theme of this book. In social ethics, just as much as in personal morals, the Christian approach is properly *God-centred*.

Even the commonly assumed distinction between 'personal' and 'social' ethics is one that threatens to melt away when God's concern with the whole of life is fully appreciated. Totalitarian states are normally quite content to tolerate a religion which deals only in person-to-person behaviour and keeps its mouth shut on social issues. Hitler's minister of propaganda, for example, warned that 'churchmen dabbling in politics should take note that their only task is to prepare for the world hereafter'. But the Bible teaches its readers that God is as interested in community affairs as He is in personal relationships, and (as we have already seen) Scripture roundly condemns the mutilated obedience offered to Him by religious people who have no social concern. Sometimes it is not even clear whether a particular command of the Bible is addressed to the individual or to the community at large. Are the 'Thou shalt nots' of the Ten Commandments, for example, meant for the individual Israelite or for the whole national community? Despite the use of the singular, the context makes the second interpretation the more likely one, but we cannot be absolutely certain, because personal and community interests intertwine so closely in Scripture.

Unlike most of his neighbours, the Old Testament believer was not dealing in his moral life with a whole team of different deities, each responsible for a different area of behaviour, giving limitless opportunities to the clever man to play one off against another. He was bound in obedience to *one* God who controlled *all* he did. One and the same divine will governed his *religious* life (when he made a sacrifice or said a prayer), his *family* life (when he married or had a child), his *working* life (when he built a house or reaped the harvest), his *political* life (when he paid his taxes or administered justice) – and any other department of life he could possibly think of. Modern practice makes an interesting contrast to this. We live today under a kind of 'moral polytheism', where different standards are accepted in different areas of life, and it is common practice to play one off against another. So a leading churchman can defend a pornographic book because of its literary merits (as though 'special' standards apply in the world of literature which do not hold elsewhere). A politician is a little hurt if others reproach him too severely for overstating his case or breaking his promises, because everyone knows that such things are all part of political life anyway. And the businessman adjusts to a different standard of truth-telling when he leaves home for his office because, after all, the man on the other end of the telephone line knows exactly what is meant when his secretary says he is 'not in'.

One could multiply such examples with little effort, but the Christian will not rest content with the smiling reassurance that 'such is life'. His God not only sanctifies but integrates every department of life. He is the God not only of the church pew and the private thought, but of the shop counter and the factory floor, of the public meeting and the office desk, of the magistrates' court and the refugee camp. And it is in the light of His all-embracing love that the whole of life must be lived, both public and private.

# PRACTISING THE PRINCIPLES

## Problem situations

One of Schulz's 'Peanuts' cartoons pictures Snoopy the dog looking distinctly unhappy in an upside-down position. 'I'm teaching him to stand on his head,' explains Charlie Brown. 'Can *you* do that?' Lucy asks incredulously. 'Oh no,' replies Charlie B., 'but those who can't do, teach.'

The jibe is an old one, but it makes an uncomfortable point when the subject under discussion is morality. The gap between ethical knowledge on the one hand and moral behaviour on the other – between teaching and learning moral theory and putting that theory into practice – is a notoriously difficult one to bridge. In the next chapter we shall be considering the dilemma man faces in trying to find within himself the strength to live up to the moral standards he theoretically accepts. But even before the stage of *doing* the right thing is reached, ordinary daily living throws up problems which are sometimes so complex that it becomes extremely hard to decide what the right course of action actually is. 'Do God's will and you will be right' may be sound theoretical advice, but in practice the circumstances of many a real-life situation make it very difficult to discover exactly what God's will does prescribe. If we go on to say, 'God reveals His will to us in the Bible, so we can be sure of pleasing Him if we behave as the Bible instructs us,' we may still find ourselves no nearer a practical solution. There are moral problems in life, big and small, for which it seems impossible to find ready-made directives in the pages of Scripture, however willing we are to learn and obey.

Broadly speaking, there are two kinds of situation in which the Christian finds it hard to come to right moral decisions. The first is when two clear moral principles of Scripture conflict. The Christian student, for example, is instructed by the Ten Commandments to honour his parents, while the New Testament tells him equally firmly that he must make time to worship God in the company of other believers. The two obligations may never clash, but if family plans on Sundays during the vacation mean that he can only rarely get to church services, and no suitable alternative arrangements can be agreed, he may find himself with a very difficult decision to take. Is he to abandon all hopes of regular corporate worship, or should he insist on going to church at the risk of a family split? Is there a biblical formula to resolve such difficulties? Or, if not, on what grounds is he to decide which is the prior duty? Life is full of such 'grey' areas of moral decision-making. As Kenneth Greet aptly puts it, 'The man who sees everything in black and white is morally colour-blind.'

Then, secondly, there are those pressing contemporary moral issues on which Christian opinion is eagerly sought, but on which the Bible has nothing directly to say. The rights and wrongs of speculation on the Stock Exchange, for example; the use of nuclear weapons in warfare, and the arrival on the market of a 'morning after' birth control pill are all subjects for keen debate, but the Bible-reader searches the Scriptures in vain to find clear guidance on these and other topics that regularly make the headlines. What *is* God's will on heart transplants or abortion clinics – or on a host of other things that cry out for a clear-cut Christian opinion?

Critics of a Bible-based morality would say, of course,

that this is an inevitable *impasse*. The relevance of teaching which is two thousand years old, directed to an occupied nation in a pre-industrialized age, is bound, they would say, to be extremely limited. To claim that the Bible must be accepted as supremely authoritative for moral living in the twentieth century seems to them about as silly as to suggest to a modern medical school that it should adopt the writings of Hippocrates as its basic textbook. To meet the moral demands of today the need is for a fresh, twentieth-century approach to morality which talks in terms of napalm burns, not about 'seething kids in their mothers' milk'. Any attempt to carry over biblical moral teaching into the very different conditions of modern life will inevitably invite misunderstanding and even disaster. How dangerous it would be, for example, if a significant number of people took the Old Testament's glowing praise of large families too seriously at a time when the world's population needs to be curbed, not increased.

The force of these charges must not be underestimated. If it can be proved that the Bible is irrelevant to the practical complexities of modern living, the whole foundation of Christian morality crumples. If we believe that the Bible reveals God's will for all men at all times, and that His will expresses what is absolutely good, then to claim that the Bible's teaching is irrelevant is tantamount to saying that God's will (and, with it, the Christian's standard of goodness) can become obsolete with the passing of time. The Bible itself flatly denies such a possibility. 'Thy kingdom', says the Psalmist, 'is an everlasting kingdom, and thy dominion endures throughout all generations' (Ps. 145: 13). By definition, the *eternal* God's sovereign will cannot date. Although no human father would expect to direct his children's behaviour beyond a certain age, the situation is different when 'father' is spelt with a capital 'F'. Man can never 'come of age' in the sense that he can outgrow his heavenly Father's moral authority. The eternal God's

85

moral standards are ever-relevant, and His moral authority coextensive with the whole of time.

Such a theological conclusion will not convince those who are not impressed by the argument of chapter 1, but there are other more obvious ways in which the relevance of biblical teaching can be demonstrated. When the Bible's moral teaching is examined as a whole, it quickly becomes apparent that its main concern is not with the local and temporal situations in which it is firmly set, but with those impulses and desires of human nature which defy the normal processes of change. Its message is directed to the Man behind every man. As someone has pointed out, a bride shares the joy, the love, the hopes and the fears of all brides at all times in all places, whether she arrives for her wedding on a camel or in a Rolls Royce. Such things are part of our common human experience. So although the external trappings of life may change, the moral categories in which the Bible deals (love, mercy, pride, vindictiveness and the rest of them) are as lasting as human nature itself. Amos' cheating tradesmen have been in their graves for many centuries, but their spirit lives on in the modern world of big business. The materialistic attitude which prompted Jesus to say 'a man's life does not consist in the abundance of his possessions' has by no means vanished from the face of the earth. To pretend that the relevance of such an ethic is limited to its original setting in Israel centuries ago is to indulge in the kind of shallow thinking Professor A. E. Taylor criticizes when he describes 'a philosophy which ignores the reality of "universal human nature" ' as 'a philosophy which does not look "under the skin" '. Man bears about with him in every century and in all places the characteristics of his humanity, and because the Bible directs itself to life at this level, its teaching will never become obsolete.

Confidence in the relevance of biblical teaching, however, still does not automatically resolve the acute problems

Christians have to face in finding out what they ought or ought not to do in the frequently very complex circumstances of modern life. Although the kernel of the Bible's moral truth is always relevant, the husk of its setting in ancient times and faraway places is sometimes difficult to pierce. And in addition to the difficulties involved in working out contemporary applications of Bible teaching, there are also the knotty problems that arise when two or more clear-cut biblical principles apparently conflict. Where should the Christian look for help in resolving moral problems on which the Bible either speaks with two voices, or seems altogether silent?

## Two conflicting answers

History provides two very different answers to this question which has perplexed men through the centuries. On one side stands the *casuist*. His solution is to *amplify* the commandments of the Bible by breaking them down into a vast network of moral by-laws, detailed enough to cover every conceivable set of circumstances in life. Perhaps the best-known exponents of casuistry in the history of the church were the Jesuits of the seventeenth century, but long before their time the scribes and Pharisees had used a similar method to interpret the moral teaching of the Old Testament. Work on the sabbath, for example, had been classified under thirty-nine different headings by Jesus' time, with the praiseworthy object of making it absolutely clear exactly what the Ten Commandments meant when they said, 'Remember the sabbath day, to keep it holy.' Detailed instructions set out the correct course of action to take if a man contracted a throat infection on the sabbath, or his wife had a baby, or a wall fell on top of his neighbour. No decision affecting behaviour was considered trivial enough to be left to the individual's own discretion, and all the by-laws were reckoned to be as binding as the biblical commandments which they set out to interpret.

It was much the same in seventeenth-century England. A devout believer could discover from his Jesuit confessor just what he should say (for example) if asked by a proud host whether he had enjoyed a particularly tasteless meal, or when questioned by an officer of the law about a crime he knew a relative had committed. No stone was left unturned in the attempt to legislate for every imaginable situation of life under the one detailed code of moral law.

Jesus' condemnation of rabbinic casuistry is potent enough to dissuade any Christian from adopting this method of solving his moral problems, and it is interesting to notice how closely criticisms of the Jesuits' methods (spearheaded by Blaise Pascal) match the charges levelled against the scribes in the Gospels. Both had fallen into the same bog of legalism, swamped by a mass of petty legislation which was so complicated that teams of 'ecclesiastical solicitors' were needed to interpret it, and so tied up with detail that the main-line moral principles were frequently lost to all sight in a mass of triviality. Worst of all, the heavy emphasis laid on the letter of the law usually meant that its spirit was totally ignored. One Jesuit writer, for example, in an attempt to define the sin of gaining ecclesiastical appointments by bribery, declared, 'It is not simony to get possession of a benefice by promising a sum of money, *when one has no intention of actually paying the money*; for this is merely making a show of simony, and is as far from being real simony as counterfeit gold is from the genuine.' 'By this quirk of conscience', comments Pascal, 'he has contrived means, in the way of adding swindling to simony, for obtaining benefices without simony and without money.' As handled by Jesuit casuistry, Christian moral law was made to condone all sorts of dubious practices (shades of the Pharisees!), including adultery and perjury. So what was meant to be a guide to help men live the moral life more surely, became a classification of excuses to ease niggling consciences.

Over against the casuist stands the *situationist* whom we have already met in chapter 2. Instead of *amplifying* the moral law of the Bible by introducing supplementary legislation, the situationist wants us to *telescope* it into a single commandment. 'The ruling norm of Christian decision', writes Joseph Fletcher, author of *Situation Ethics*, 'is LOVE; nothing else.' Fletcher damns the casuist with faint praise. Casuistry, he explains, is the legalist's way out of the web he has woven to choke himself. It is what happens when a law ethic tries to listen to the voice of love and rise above its legalism. If a homicidal maniac arrives on my doorstep and asks whether my wife is in, the impersonal letter of the law insists 'You must tell him the truth'. The casuist, though a legalist at heart, recognizes the impossibility of such a situation in human terms, so he adds a compromising codicil: 'You must tell the truth – unless it would cost a life.' It is to the casuist's credit, Fletcher suggests, that he is prepared to soften the harshness of law by creating a new rule to break the old, but the price he has to pay in hypocrisy and doublethink is a terrible one. The situationist, on the other hand, is thankfully free from all pre-set rules and regulations. He can make use of the old moral 'laws', but only to advise him and never to dictate his decisions. Consequently he is quite free to discover for himself the way of love in any situation, however complex it may be.

If at this point the objection is raised that Jesus Himself appears to have given His disciples some specific moral instructions as well as the general command to love, the situationist has his answer ready. We misunderstand Jesus, he explains, if we think He meant us to obey His ethical commands to the letter. Even on those occasions when He appears to be laying down firm moral laws, His intention was never to strait-jacket us with a set of rules and regulations, but only to provide broad guiding principles to help us in shaping our attitudes. So when He said, 'Give to him who begs from you,' He did not mean that we should invariably reward *every* beggar who rings the doorbell; it was just His vivid way of saying, 'Be generous.' We are not necessarily disobeying a command of Jesus, therefore, if we decide *not* to give on a particular occasion (providing, of course, that we are generous by disposition and have a loving reason for refusing). Similarly, the straightforward Gospel commands not to indulge in extra-marital sex are not meant to be interpreted as absolute prohibitions. Jesus' concern was to teach *the basic Christian attitude* towards sexual relationships – that they should not be entered upon (or opted out of) lightly. Fletcher gives examples of situations in which considerations of love may lead a man to fornicate or commit adultery, and in such circumstances, he says, the Christian need feel no twinges of conscience when he follows love's leading boldly.

Although the situationist's promise to rescue us from the clammy trap of casuistry is attractive, this is by no means a convincing exposition of Jesus' moral teaching. 'It is on a deductive theory from the concept of love,' concludes Michael Ramsey, Archbishop of Canterbury, in a penetrating analysis of situation ethics, 'and not upon a full examination of Christ's teaching, that the conclusion is being drawn that "nothing of itself can be labelled as wrong".'[1] In other words, the situationist has fallen into the trap of manipulating the Bible to suit his ethical theory, instead of working the other way round. To his credit, Fletcher is quite frank about his approach to the Bible. On divorce, for example, he writes: 'The fact that Jesus is reported in the Gospels as having . . . absolutized the prohibition of divorce, poses a problem for biblical scholarship (especially troublesome to the literalizers and legalists) but it does not confuse Christian ethics, at least of the situationist stamp.' Such a

[1] A. M. Ramsey, *Image Old and New* (SPCK, 1963), p. 14.

cavalier approach to the New Testament may not bother the situationist, but it will cause deep concern to the Christian who aims to follow the teaching of Jesus at all closely. It seems clear that Jesus expected His specific moral demands to be taken far more seriously than the situationist will allow.

If, then, the *situationist* sits too loose to the commands of Jesus, and the *casuist* makes the mistake of trying to fill the gaps in God's law by introducing a mass of new rules and regulations, the modern disciple has somehow to drive a middle course between the two. Can a way be found which respects the important role of law, while still making room for the flexibility which Scripture allows the individual in making his own moral decisions?

## The Bible and contemporary issues

In feeling our way cautiously towards a middle course, let us first look again at the difficulties involved in *applying* the Bible's teaching to modern issues. Problems of application are fundamentally problems of interpretation. The would-be Bible teacher has it drummed into him during training that 'a text without a context is a pretext', and we know how easily neglect of this basic principle can spoil the best-intended attempts to arrive at a truly biblical theology. The same is true in the ethical field. Failure to give full weight to the context in which a particular piece of moral teaching is set has led in the past to some extremely dubious applications of biblical ethics. We have already noticed how heavily advocates of the monastic life leaned on Jesus' words to the rich young ruler, 'Sell what you have'. What some of them ignored was the fact that Jesus gave this instruction to an *individual*, and it is highly dangerous to assume that what He demanded of one man He demands of all who aspire to be fully dedicated Christians. The context helps us to see this kind of radical demand in its proper perspective (in this case, a call to whole-hearted discipleship). In a similar way, there are some pacifists who point to Jesus' words in the Sermon on the Mount, 'Do not resist one who is evil,' as a conclusive proof-text for their case. They fail to notice that the context of this command in Matthew 5 has to do with *personal relationships*, not with international affairs. Tolstoy went so far as to use this verse to press for the abolition of the state's police force – one of the more bizarre illustrations of the perils involved in taking a text out of context when trying to apply biblical teaching to contemporary issues.

All this, however, is rather negative. As well as preventing careless applications of Bible verses, a clear understanding of the context of a particular commandment will often shed valuable light on its full purpose and meaning for today. The so-called '*lex talionis*' of the Old Testament (the law which demanded 'an eye for an eye and a tooth for a tooth') is a good case in point. To take the wording of this law at its face value today would be courting social disaster. It would encourage the vindictive 'tit for tat' spirit of Mafia-style vendettas, the spiteful, unforgiving attitude to others which Jesus so forthrightly condemns in the Gospels. But to interpret the '*lex talionis*' in this way at all is really to treat it unbiblically, because its original setting in Exodus calls for quite a different interpretation. When it was first laid down, it had two very constructive aims; in the first place to take away the right of exacting retribution from the individual and give it to the courts (so that *two* eyes were not taken for one); and secondly to fix guidelines for the courts in assessing just sentences and fair damages.[2] Seen in its proper setting, then, this piece of ancient law still has its relevance today. Even the spirit of its wording has passed across into modern social legislation. Some vehicle insurance

[2] The fact that the law's provisions are to be taken as guidelines only is made clear by the context; see Ex. 21: 26, 27.

policies, for example, still contain the phrase 'knock for knock', which is presumably not meant to encourage the car owner to take the law into his own hands, but is accepted, nevertheless, as a fair basis for settling accident claims.[3]

Perhaps the most important reason for setting Bible laws in their right contexts is that only in this way can the Christian distinguish between those moral commandments which are intended to be applied universally (binding on all men at all times in all places), and others which have just temporary or local significance. Sometimes the distinction is obvious. The sacrificial laws of the Old Testament, for instance, became redundant after the death of Christ; and much of Israel's civil law is geared to the social and political conditions of the day which now no longer apply. In other cases, however, it is not nearly so easy to see whether the full force of a biblical command is meant to apply today or not. To take promiscuity as an example, it is sometimes argued that the Bible's strict prohibition of extra-marital sex is one of those pieces of moral teaching which must be seen against the background of the conditions of its time. It was a necessary safeguard against venereal disease and unwanted babies in Bible times, we are told, but with the arrival of antibiotics and reliable contraceptives it no longer has a useful purpose to serve and can therefore safely be shelved. Only a careful examination of the way this teaching is phrased reveals that the main argument the Bible uses against sexual intercourse outside marriage is not based on disease or unwanted pregnancies at all, but on the damage such behaviour causes to the *human personality* (*cf.* 1 Cor. 6: 18, where the word 'body' has much more than a physical significance). The discovery of better antibiotics and safer contraceptives is therefore hardly relevant to the moral case the Bible presents. It rests, in fact, on a far deeper foundation, the nature of man as

[3] F. D. Kidner's illustration in *Hard Sayings* (IVP, 1972), p. 37.

God created him, and is therefore as relevant today as it was in New Testament times.

Even those laws of the Bible which cannot be directly applied today, because of changed social conditions, do not lose their relevance altogether. Most of them are themselves applications of major moral principles which are still valuable guides to conduct, once their setting in time and place is fully appreciated. The Old Testament instruction to householders, for example, to 'put a parapet along the roof when you build a new house' obviously cannot apply very widely in a society where flat-roofed houses are rarely built, but the principle of *public safety* which it expresses should still influence local authorities when they decide whether or not to give planning permission to new building projects. We have a New Testament example of the same thing in the middle of the Sermon on the Mount, when Jesus follows up His command 'Do not resist one who is evil' with three specific illustrations of what he means by non-resistance: 'if any one strikes you on the right cheek, turn to him the other also; and if any one would sue you and take your coat, let him have your cloak as well; and if any one forces you to go one mile, go with him two miles'. Modern suburban-dwellers may live the whole of their lives without getting involved in any one of these crisis situations, but that does not exempt them from the force of Jesus' teaching. The main principle behind the illustrations still holds good (and in this case is clearly spelled out), and it is the modern disciple's duty to work out its right application in the particular life-situations in which *he* finds himself.

It was in this spirit that the Old Testament prophets set about applying the covenant law to the moral issues of their own day. We sometimes forget that the Old Testament spans many centuries, and by the time the prophets came on the scene in the eighth century before Christ, social conditions had radically altered from the wilderness days when Moses received the law on Mount Sinai. Amos' contemporaries lived in summer-houses and winter-houses, not in tents. Big business flourished. There was speculation and money-lending on a large scale in the markets. Alliances and cultural exchanges were arranged with foreign powers, and the old insistence that money and possessions were symbols of God's blessing had given way to a frankly materialistic attitude to life. The law of the covenant seemed to have very little to say in such an alien cultural environment, but the prophets set to work with such vigour to bring out its contemporary relevance that they soon had society by its ears, and the well-heeled representatives of all the vested interests in the land howling for their blood.

One is tempted to conclude that it is the lack of such 'prophetic application' today which is responsible for the widespread bewilderment Christians feel when they are faced by the challenge of contemporary moral issues. It does not matter very much that words like 'euthanasia' and 'strike' do not feature in the Bible's vocabulary. The mainline principles for directing personal and social conduct in God's way are still to be found in Scripture, and they are still relevant. The need is for more prophetic voices to interpret those principles accurately, and to apply them with vigour.

## Clashes of principle

In the remaining few pages of this chapter, we must turn our attention to the second main area of perplexity Christians feel in trying to use the Bible's moral teaching in a practical way. If anything is more difficult than discovering God's will about things on which the Bible has nothing to say, it must surely be to know His will on those occasions when (apparently) the Bible says too much. The airman who is ordered to drop bombs on a village, for instance, is caught in a biblical crossfire. One voice from Scripture tells him that human life is sacrosanct. Another says, 'He who resists the authorities resists what God has appointed.' If he observes the one principle he will disobey the other. It seems that the best he can do in the situation is something Scripture condemns. In Thomas Jefferson's words, quoted by Lyndon Johnson in his 'State of the Union' message of 1966, 'It is sometimes the melancholy duty of human societies to engage in some great evil in order to ward off a greater.'

If it does not offer an immediate solution to this kind of problem, it is nevertheless encouraging to discover that the Bible itself recognizes the need to make these 'lesser evil' choices. If we take the issue of divorce, for example, the Bible is quite explicit about God's ideal marriage standards: 'Therefore a man leaves his father and his mother and cleaves to his wife' (Gn. 2: 24). Jesus quoted these words and concluded 'No divorce' (Mk. 10: 6–12). Writing later to the church at Corinth, with Jesus' teaching in mind, Paul draws the same conclusion (1 Cor. 7: 10). But both Paul and Jesus recognize that in some human situations God's ideal standard simply cannot be reached. Sometimes a marriage relationship may be so broken that separation or divorce becomes the lesser evil (Mt. 19: 9; 1 Cor. 7: 15). Looking back to the Old Testament divorce law, Jesus reminded His hearers that it was to cope with human 'hardness of heart' that Moses introduced legislation for the irretrievable breakdown of marriage; and because men's hearts have not grown any softer, sin still makes the divorce law a social necessity. This does not mean that God's standards change. He still 'hates divorce' (Mal. 2: 16), and divorce is therefore still an evil. But although bad, it may nevertheless not be quite so bad as any available alternative in some situations.

This point highlights another clash with the situationist.

Joseph Fletcher quotes a passage from Alexander Miller's *Renewal of Man*, in which the author describes an interview he had with members of the French *maquis* after World War II. The Frenchmen had lived on lies and theft for four years; they had killed occupation officers, collaborators, and sometimes even their own comrades in order to avoid betrayal. Miller defends their activities, a little uncomfortably, as *lesser-evil* choices. 'If killing and lying are to be used,' he concludes, 'it must be under the most urgent pressure of social necessity, and with a profound sense of guilt that no better way can presently be found.' For Fletcher, however, 'guilt' is much too strong a word to use. If love dictates that a man kills or tells a lie, he is doing something *good* (not something excusably bad) when he complies, according to the situationist. As Fletcher writes elsewhere, 'If a lie is told unlovingly, it is wrong, evil; if it is told in love it is good, right. . . . Love makes it good.'

One cannot help thinking that at this point Miller's view is more biblical than Fletcher's. The Bible clearly distinguishes good actions from bad ones. It also agrees that there are times when, on the 'lesser evil' principle, it may regrettably be *right* to do something *bad*, because there is no better alternative. But in these cases the bad does not automatically become *good* because it is the right thing to do in the circumstances. And this is not such a hair-splitting argument as it may sound. To say that telling a lie or taking a life can ever be *good* things to do is dangerously misleading, because it encourages a frame of mind in which the sense of *badness* these things should always convey is greatly weakened, or even lost. *Bad* they are, and *bad* they remain. William Barclay draws a helpful parallel with the use of dangerous drugs in medicine. When a doctor prescribes them, he does not pretend that these drugs automatically lose all their poisonous properties because they are being used as medicines. 'Poisons they are and poisons they remain. They have to be kept in a special cupboard and in a special container. They can only be used under the strictest safeguards. . . . These things have a kind of inbuilt red light and that red light is not taken away, for the dangerous drug is never called anything else but a poison. So there are certain things which on rare occasions may be used to serve a good end. But the red light should not be removed by calling them good things. They remain highly dangerous, and they should never be called, or regarded as, anything else.'[4]

Any lesser-evil (or, for that matter, greater-good) choice involves selecting between moral obligations, and this in turn implies a grading of responsibilities so that greater duties can be set above lesser. Thus a gynaecologist may recommend an abortion for a mother-to-be whose life is in danger, while refusing to operate on another girl who is simply unwilling to go through with her pregnancy, on the grounds that the value of a foetus' life must be set below that of a woman's physical safety but above that of her personal convenience. In a similar way a Christian Trade Union member, before he responds to a strike-call, will want to weigh the nature and importance of the grievance very carefully against the disruption strike-action would cause; he has to place his responsibilities (to his firm, to his workmates, and to all third parties concerned) in some kind of order, before he can make a right moral decision.

Distasteful though this 'league-table' approach to morality may sound, it is one that the Bible strongly encourages us to adopt. One of the Pharisees' most fatal mistakes, according to Jesus, was to get their morality tables upside down. To change the metaphor, they concentrated so much on the small print of the moral law that they neglected its main thrust *which was more important*. They were so preoccupied with the tithing of their herb-gardens that they became guilty of neglecting the 'weightier

⁴ W. Barclay, *Ethics in a Permissive Society* (Collins Fontana, 1971), p. 82.

matters of the law, justice and mercy and faith' (Mt. 23:23). It was not that they were wrong to extend the tithing principle to their tiniest possessions ('these things you ought to have done'). Their fault lay in setting this kind of minor obligation above other much more important considerations in their scale of moral priorities. In Jesus' vivid phrase, which must have sent a ripple of laughter around his audience, they were guilty of 'straining out a gnat and swallowing a camel!'.

The New Testament is rich in its illustrations of this obligation-grading principle at work. At Rome, for example, the church was split on the question of eating meat that had been sacrificed to idols. Some said, 'Christians ought to leave this meat alone, because eating it compromises their witness.' Others disagreed. 'Christians should eat it openly,' they argued, 'to demonstrate their belief that idols count for nothing.' It is interesting that instead of trying to decide between these two views on merit, Paul's solution is to remind both parties of a *higher* moral obligation which must be allowed to override their disagreement: 'Let us then pursue what makes for peace and for mutual upbuilding' (Rom. 14:19). In other words, unity among church members must be put above the rights and wrongs of food and drink in the scale of Christian priorities. We can see the same principle at work in the 'compromise' decision of the Council of Jerusalem in Acts 15. The problem was whether to admit Gentiles to the church without insisting on their observing the ceremonial of the Jewish law. Arguments were raised on both sides. Finally it was agreed that Gentile converts should not be subject to the requirements of Jewish ceremonial – *but that they should nevertheless eat their food 'kosher'*. Soon this condition was dropped too, but in the meantime the conscientious scruples of some about food laws must be respected, if only to cement unity within the church – which was so much more important a consideration. So we find Paul himself circumcising Timothy and financing a group of men about to take Nazirite vows (Acts 16: 3; 21: 17ff.), although we know full well from the Epistles the strong views he held about the value of circumcision and Jewish law observance. It was all a matter of priorities, and in this case evangelism took precedence over all other considerations in Paul's opinion.

The verdict of history may well be that Christians today are not as good as they should be at making this kind of lesser-evil judgment. We find it very hard to live in non-ideal situations. We may fight shy of becoming involved in such areas of life as politics or the entertainment world where the Christian cannot hope to put everything right at once, and therefore must constantly rest content with lesser-evil choices. In any life-situation it is much easier to opt out and do nothing than to shelve one biblical principle in order to achieve another, if only because this kind of strategy smacks so strongly of compromise and will certainly be interpreted as such by some. Yet the Bible gives us every encouragement to take these 'lesser-evil' and 'greater-good' decisions. It does not leave us with the impression that the process of choosing will be easy, but with his Bible open and fortified by the promise that the Holy Spirit will direct the minds of those who are open to His instruction, the Christian can make these difficult moral judgments with confidence. As the Epistle to the Hebrews puts it, mature Christians are those who, feeding on the 'solid food' of God's Word, 'have their faculties trained by practice to distinguish good from evil' (Heb. 5: 14).

# POWER THROUGH CHRIST

The ultimate test of any ethical theory is its power to turn ideas into actions. A moral standard that is completely beyond the average man's capacity to keep may have its value in keeping him humble, but for the practical purposes of daily living it is virtually useless. And such a 'practicability test' is all the more vital because man's chief difficulty in living the moral life lies not so much in making his mind up about the right things to do, even in the kind of complex situations described in the last chapter, but in finding within himself the strength of moral will-power to carry his decisions into practice. It may be possible to convince somebody that a certain course of action is right. It will be much harder to instil into him a sense of urgency that he ought to do it *now*, and to provide him with the moral dynamic to convert the conviction into action. As Jesus pointed out in His story about the two sons who were asked to work in their father's vineyard, there is a world of difference between recognizing a moral duty and acting upon it. 'If you *know* these things,' He told His disciples, 'blessed are you if you *do* them' (Jn. 13: 17).

It is at this very practical level that most of the major moral battles of life are fought. An ethics teacher may find it hard to get an audience to listen to his theories, but once he can point to changed lives among his disciples the world will sit up and take notice. The testimony of a cured drug-addict, for example, or of an alcoholic who has found the way to 'turn drink into furniture', will carry far more weight than a whole series of eloquent addresses from the lecture desk. This was undoubtedly why the impact the first Christians made on their neighbours was out of all proportion to their numerical strength.

In the first letter that Paul wrote to the Corinthians, he catalogues the vices any casual visitor to the city of Corinth might meet – 'adulterers, homosexuals, thieves, the greedy, drunkards, revilers, robbers'. '*And such*', he reminds his Christian readers, '*were some of you*' (1 Cor. 6: 11). The Christians at Corinth were demonstrating by their changed lives the moral potency of the Christian gospel, and inevitably their friends and neighbours wanted to know what had made the difference. At a community level, too, the early church showed by its compassionate love-life how age-old barriers of race, class and sex could be smashed. It was all very impressive. When the news percolated through to Rome, the emperor Julian wrote to Arsacius complaining rather peevishly, 'The godless Galileans nourish *our* poor in addition to their own; while ours get no care from us.'

The picture was not an altogether rosy one, of course, as is only too clear from Paul's letters. At Corinth, as elsewhere, ugly moral failures stood out like blots on the bright success stories. There were bitter personal rivalries which threatened the church's community life and blatant breaches of basic moral standards that spoiled its witness to outsiders. And the situation at Corinth was unfortunately by no means unique in this respect. No period of Christian history has been without its moral blemishes, and there will always be plenty of evidence to make men like Bertrand Russell sigh, 'The trouble with Christ was that He had disciples.' Nevertheless, the fact that a church leader's moral failings are still considered newsworthy enough to make the headlines supports Lecky's verdict, in his *History of European Morals*, that the Christian gospel is 'the most powerful moral lever that has ever been applied to the affairs of men'. As every Christian knows, other people expect him not only to believe in, but also to *live up to*, the high moral standards he professes, and that in itself is an unspoken compliment to the moral power the Christian gospel is still assumed to have.

## Failure without tears

Compliment or not, such an assumption cuts right across the spirit of the times. The level of moral integrity we have come to expect in, for example, the business world or the cut and thrust of political life is very low. However high the standard a man, or a firm, may profess, we do not really expect him (or them) to achieve it consistently, and if we are at all realistic we make allowances accordingly. We live in an age of moral pessimism, when it seems that all the bridges that have been built across the gulf between moral theory and practice are in a state of collapse. The old humanist dream that selfishness, cruelty and all the other barriers to man's moral progress would disappear with the advance of education now seems as naive as Socrates' belief that a man will automatically do what is good when he clearly understands what it involves. Perhaps the Roman poet Ovid showed a deeper appreciation of human nature than the Greek philosopher when he confessed: 'I see and approve what is better, but I follow what is worse.' The world is not short of good moral theory, but experience has taught us that although certain cruder forms of wrong-doing may be eliminated by better education, they are replaced only too often by more refined and subtle forms which are even more deadly. And the Christian is not surprised to find that things work out this way. Education, he would point out, is powerless to ensure good living, because ignorance is not the root cause of sin.

It is possible, of course, to paint too black a picture of contemporary moral behaviour, and Christians are sometimes too glib in making their gloomy analyses of modern trends. Although the jump in the divorce rate, for example, is enough to alarm anyone who believes that family life is worth preserving, the statistics may prove little more than that more dead marriages are now receiving a proper burial, due to changes in social conventions and the law of the land. Two prominent sociologists, Ferdyn and Zweig, have argued that factors like better housing, higher earnings and less drunkenness have made home life *more* stable now than it was in Victorian times. Again, evidence that one live birth in twenty is illegitimate may appal us, but comparison with the figures for a hundred years ago shows that the illegitimacy rate has actually gone *down* since then (though only by 0.9 per cent). The Victorians may have viewed unchastity with displeasure, but they obviously had to view it fairly frequently.

Such points are worth making, but only as wise cautions against overstating a case which needs no exaggeration. The world abounds in good advice, as it always has done, but in spite of all the fine ideals, the problem of man's incapacity to do the good he knows he ought to do remains no nearer solution. Hence the modern disillusionment with ideas of a moral and political utopia, so confidently predicted by a long chain of optimists stretching back from H. G. Wells to Plato. Modern visionaries like Aldous Huxley and George Orwell are openly pessimistic about moral progress. The world they foresee is not one in which good triumphs over evil, but very much the opposite.

Oddly enough, very little *pain* or *distress* seems to be attached to this recognition of moral failure; and, appropriately, it is the men of medicine who are responsible for administering the best moral anaesthetics. Regard your shortcomings as inevitable, we are told, and they will stop bothering you. The best cure for a troubled conscience is to understand *why* you fail, and then you will stop worrying about it.

Research has shown how closely an individual's behaviour is bound up with his health, physical and mental. Gland disturbance, for example, can account for a man's disloyalty to his wife; and diseases of old age, such as hardening of the arteries, may reveal themselves in behaviour traits such as suspicion and jealousy, along with the more obviously physical symptoms. Sexual anomalies, too, which may involve children and result in trouble with the law, probably have hidden physical causes. 'We would suggest', write Henderson and Gillespie in their *Textbook of Psychiatry*, 'that in all persons over the age of fifty years accused for the first time of sexual offences, the possibility of beginning organic brain disease should always be suspected.' No-one would argue that such conduct is good, or that society should not pass laws to protect children, but the question arises as to whether the wrong-doer in such a case is morally responsible for his actions. What he has done is undoubtedly *bad*, but is he to *blame*? To reproach a man for behaviour which is symptomatic of an illness seems as illogical as finding fault with a child for having spots when he has caught measles.

Psychologists have extended this principle to cover circumstances of life which would be considered far too normal to claim the doctor's attention. Factors such as heredity and environment, for example, have long been recognized as exercising a formidable influence on behaviour, and the individual can no more opt out of these pressures than he can refuse to have a swollen face when he is suffering from mumps. So once again, if the question is asked, 'Is X to *blame* for acting in the way he has been conditioned to behave?' we are encouraged to answer in the negative. When the statistics show that anyone living in a city slum is twenty times more likely to be convicted of an offence than someone brought up in a more 'desirable' residential area, it is hard to argue that equal blame must attach to offenders from both communities. If blame is to be apportioned at all, it lies with society, not with the individual. In Kafka's words, modern man pleads, 'I am not guilty; it's a misunderstanding. And if it comes to that, how can *any* man be called guilty?'

Within the pessimistic streak which runs through contemporary moral thinking, then, there is this feeling of helpless complacency which draws the sting from moral failure. If we are all in the grip of pressures we cannot fully control, is it not illogical to have a bad conscience about anything? After all, no-one can be blamed for failing to live a moral life which is beyond his capabilities. Canon Fenton Morley, in a sermon preached in Leeds University Church not long after an undergraduate had been sent down from Oxford for immoral behaviour, showed how even the old titles of the seven deadly sins have succumbed to the influence of conscience sedatives prescribed by the obliging psychiatrist. 'We have turned *pride* into self-fulfilment,' he said, '*envy* into insecurity, *anger* into stress, *avarice* into the pursuit of incentives, *sloth* into constitutional inertia, *gluttony* into defective metabolism, and *lust* into emotional tension.' Translated into such terms, old-fashioned sin calls for sympathetic understanding, not for stern condemnation. As the French would say, '*Tout comprendre est tout pardonner.*'

The Bible goes along with the psychologist's diagnosis, but not with all his conclusions. There can be few clearer statements of man's moral helplessness in the face of pressures he cannot control than Paul's frank admission in Romans 7: 18 – 'I can will what is right, but I cannot do it'; and the Old Testament, too, is quite explicit about the way sin's power travels down the generations (see, for example, Ex. 20: 5). But nowhere in the Bible, in the Old Testament or the New, is there a suggestion that the individual who commits sin because of this hereditary taint can therefore shelve his guilt on his ancestry. Similarly, the Bible's idea of group responsibility is not that the individual can *escape* responsibility for what he does by pleading 'the pressures of his environment', but rather that he must *share* the corporate guilt of the society of which he is a member. In other words, if the psychologist says, 'You are a victim of circumstances, therefore you are not to be blamed,' the Bible replies, 'As a member of your race and your society, the guilt is yours to share.'

## Power to do right

It is not, however, only the fact of corporate responsibility which makes it impossible for the individual to shelve his guilt when he does wrong. The Bible sets out an even more compelling reason why he cannot escape blame. In Christ, according to the New Testament, there is a source of super-human moral strength which will enable any man to rise above the influences of his environment and of his past. To draw a far from perfect analogy, it may be hard to blame a man for failing to undo a tight screw if he has no tools, but if he is given a power-assisted screwdriver and still insists on using his finger-nails, he cannot expect much sympathy. In a similar way, although it may sound harsh (especially in an individualistically-minded age) to call a man to account for something he has been conditioned to do by his heredity and environment, it is completely reasonable to expect him to make full use of the moral resources that are available to him to counter those pressures. And if the New Testament is to be trusted, he can find in Jesus Christ all the resources of moral energy he needs to overcome the pressures of both the past and the present. If he deliberately turns his back on a power-source like that, it is hard to see how he can escape full responsibility for the moral failures which will inevitably follow.

This takes us right to the heart of biblical ethics. The

really distinctive difference Jesus Christ made to man's moral world was not to say 'You *must*' more sternly than anyone else, but to promise 'With Me, you *can*'. If this were merely an invitation to self-hypnosis, an encouragement to persuade ourselves that we can live beyond our moral capacity, we might well prefer the more realistic approach of twentieth-century pessimism. But the promise rests on surer ground than that. Jesus Himself was fond of using 'kingdom' language to illustrate His teaching. As we have already noticed, the word 'kingdom' in the Gospels normally means 'rule' rather than 'realm', so that being in God's kingdom means living under His rule and doing His will. But Jesus' call to 'enter the kingdom of God' was much more than a summons to unconditional surrender. As well as a demand for total obedience, it was an invitation to *share the King's power*. The guidance and strength of the King are immediately available to those who put themselves under His rule. They have the light they need to make right moral decisions, and the strength they need to carry them into practice. That was why Jesus could set His moral standards so high. He was addressing those who were already 'in the kingdom', and together with the uncompromising demands went the promise of supernatural strength. There was no need for them to dilute His standards, as others have done since, to the point where the power of God is virtually unnecessary to keep them. Living in the kingdom spells an end to moral impotence.

The other New Testament writers do not use 'kingdom' language nearly so much, but they lay the same stress as Jesus did on the availability of superhuman guidance and strength to overcome moral powerlessness. No-one could accuse Paul, for example, of unfounded optimism in his moral teaching. He spends three whole chapters at the beginning of his Epistle to the Romans drawing out the sheer inevitability of moral failure. Man, he concludes, is morally a hopeless case, impotent to do good, perverted and enslaved by sin; his moral judgment is warped and his will crippled. But, thankfully, that is not the end of the story. There was just one moral teacher who not only influenced and inspired his pupils, but perfectly embodied all the high standards he taught – Jesus Christ. And Jesus not only lived a life without sin Himself, but overcame the power of evil on the cross and is alive today to feed His resurrection strength to those who lack it. This was the moral force of the gospel Paul preached. Those who acknowledge their moral powerlessness, repent of their moral failure, and surrender themselves to His will, are united with Him. In Paul's words, they find themselves 'in Christ', and in Him they discover genuine freedom from all the destructive influences of temperament and upbringing, and the cumulative effects of past failures. *Genuine* freedom does not just mean freedom to *do* something (though modern freedom-fighters sometimes give that impression), but freedom *not* to do it, and it is here that human will-power is so pitifully weak. In Christ, claims Paul, a man can break free from all the ingrained habits of the past and the pressures of the present which otherwise threaten to master his behaviour. To describe such new-found moral freedom as 'turning over a new leaf' is woefully inadequate. It is nothing less than starting a new life. 'If any one is in Christ, he is a new creation; the old has passed away, behold, the new has come' (2 Cor. 5: 17).

Living 'in Christ' (or 'in the kingdom'), then, arms the Christian with new power to do what he knows to be right. And in the New Testament such power is always associated with the presence of the Holy Spirit. The man or woman who is 'in Christ' is indwelt by the Spirit of Christ, and the indwelling Spirit is the Christian's moral dynamic. Jesus, we are told, returned 'in the power of the Spirit' from His successful battle with the devil in the desert (Lk. 4: 14), and it is the same power of the Spirit which enables the Christian to win the fight against those forces of human nature which 'prevent you from doing what you would' (Gal. 5: 16, 17).

The Holy Spirit offers to all men the strength they lack by nature to cross the broad gap between profession and practice, to turn ethical theory into practical moral living. To use Paul's words again, 'God is at work in you, both to *will* and to *work* for his good pleasure' (Phil. 2: 13).

The power of the Spirit is all-sufficient and inexhaustible, but the Bible is careful not to leave us with the impression that the man who acknowledges his moral impotence and places himself under God's rule can settle down to live out the rest of his moral life effortlessly 'on automatic'. That is not the case at all. God renovates the personality, but He does not obliterate it. He supplies all the necessary potential for moral victory, but the battles with the forces of heredity and environment still have to be fought, and some of them are very hard to win.

Peter's experience in the early days of the church's missionary expansion provides a good example of how tightly old habits can cling to the most dedicated of lives. Brought up as a strict racialist, Peter the Jew would have no dealings with Gentiles – until, that is, the Holy Spirit taught him by a vision and a visit that there are no racial partitions in God's kingdom. Peter won a famous victory that day. 'You yourselves know how unlawful it is for a Jew to associate with or to visit any one of another nation,' he testified; 'but God has shown me that I should not call any man common or unclean' (Acts 10: 28). It was a brave stand; but old attitudes die hard, and the powers of inherited prejudices are strong. So it was only a little while later, Paul tells us in his letter to the Galatians, that Peter succumbed to temptation and excused himself from Gentile hospitality while a strict Jewish delegation was in town. The pressures of heredity, in a hostile environment, proved to be too much for him.

Most Christians could match Peter's failure from their own experience. Old moral weaknesses do not disappear overnight. But through all the failures comes the persistent